PENGUIN B[

RIOT AFTER RIOT

M.J. AKBAR, an Indian Muslim, was born in January 1951. His maternal grandfather, Mir Habibullah, was a Kashmiri who took his shawl business to Amritsar. In the chaos of 1947, Amritsar was emptied of Muslims and the family went as penniless refugees to Pakistan. His paternal grandfather was orphaned early in life, and ran away from the poverty of his village in Bihar to the industrial outskirts of Calcutta. A Hindu called Prayaag, he later converted to Islam and took the name Sheikh Rahamatullah. He remained in India because of his commitment to the Congress Party.

M.J. Akbar was educated at the Calcutta Boys' School and graduated with honours in English from Presidency College, Calcutta, in 1970. He then became a trainee sub-editor with the Times of India organization and was posted to the *Illustrated Weekly of India* under Khushwant Singh. He was given the job of editing the fortnightly magazine *Onlooker* of the Free Press Journal Group in 1974 and joined the Ananda Bazar Group of Publications in Calcutta in 1976. Here he reshaped and edited the successful weekly magazine *Sunday*. In 1982, he conceived, designed and edited the new daily English newspaper of the group, *The Telegraph*, which soon achieved great success. Apart from editing these two publications, the author has also undertaken a great many on-the-spot reports and interviews. In 1985, he wrote *India: The Siege Within* which was published by Penguin. M.J. Akbar lives in Calcutta.

M.J.AKBAR

RIOT AFTER RIOT

Reports on Caste and Communal
Violence in India

PENGUIN BOOKS

Penguin Books (India) Limited, 72-B Himalaya House, 23 Kasturba Gandhi Marg,
New Delhi-110 001, India
Penguin Books Ltd., Harmondsworth, Middlesex, England
Viking Penguin Inc., 40 West 23rd Street, New York, N.Y.10010. U.S.A.
Penguin Books Australia Ltd., Ringwood, Victoria, Australia
Penguin Books Canada Ltd., 2801 John Street, Markham, Ontario, Canada L3R 1B4
Penguin Books (N.Z.) Ltd., 182-190 Wairau Road, Auckland 10, New Zealand

First published by Penguin Books India 1988

The essays in this book first appeared in *Sunday* magazine and *The Telegraph*,
Calcutta.

Made and printed in India by
Ananda Offset Private Ltd.
Typeset in Times Roman

To Aveek
With gratitude
In friendship

Contents

Introduction

The theme of this book is violence in the land of Gandhi. The Mahatma had made non-violence (*ahimsa*) an article of personal faith and forged passive resistance to injustice into a powerful political weapon. Practitioners of passive resistance were required to abjure falsehood and embrace truth: the Hindi word *Satyagrahi* (*Satya* + *Agrahi*) means one who has attached himself to the truth. A *Satyagrahi* was further enjoined to exorcise hatred from his heart : hate kills the man who hates, said the Mahatma. And added : hate the evil not the evil-doer; replace hate with love and compassion because love, as the adage goes, conquers all. Foul means can never justify fair ends : both ends and means must be equally just. Anyone who wanted to live these needed to adhere strictly to just one principle: truth above all, above truth, truthful conduct. It is enshrined in India's national motto *Satyamev Jayate* — only truth triumphs.

The Mahatma lived long enough to see his dream of a Ram Rajya (the Indian utopia) turn into one long nightmare. During the British Raj he had seen Hindu-Muslim riots break out in different cities. He believed they were engineered by the British in pursuance of their policy of divide and rule and that no sooner they were driven out than the two communities would learn to live in peace and harmony. Although it is true that these riots took place largely during Hindu or Muslim festivals, and especially when Hindu religious processions with bands of musicians and slogan-yelling crowds passed mosques where Muslims were at prayer, there is no truth in the allegation that they were engineered by the British. On the contrary, their presence as the third, neutral party prevented the police from taking sides. The riots were quickly controlled and the loss of life and property was not very alarming. It was only during the last years of the Raj that Hindu-Muslim conflicts achieved the proportions of civil wars in which people were killed by the thousands. The "Direct Action Day" in Calcutta in 1946 triggered off riots which went on for many months. It sparkled off worse violence in Bihar where Hindu mobs destroyed Muslim villages; and in Noakhali in East Bengal Muslim hoodlums settled scores on behalf of their Bihari co-religionists by killing hapless Hindus. By the spring of 1947 the North-West Frontier and the Punjab were enveloped in flames of communal strife. In this insane, hate-filled atmosphere, the only voice of sanity which was listened to with respect was that of Mahatma Gandhi. Single handedly he brought peace to Calcutta. While India and Pakistan were celebrating their independence, he was trudging from village to village in Noakhali exhorting people to abjure violence. His next pilgrimage for peace was to be to the Punjab. But by then the Punjab had been divided and millions of Sikhs and Hindus were fleeing Pakistan to come to India and an equal number of Muslims were fleeing India to go to Pakistan. It is estimated that in the two months following the partition of the country ten million people had been rendered homeless and almost half-a-million were dead.

It was about this time that the Mahatma made his final effort to stem the tide of hatred that was sweeping across the country. This was in Delhi in the autumn of 1947 when Hindu and Sikh refugees from Pakistan were hell-bent on driving the Muslims out of Delhi. Once again, and again single-handed, it was the Mahatma who through his fast to atone for the wrongs done to innocent Muslims converted hate-mongers into peace-loving citizens. A few days later, on 30 January, 1948 he paid the price of fearlessly treading the path of truth and non-violence with his own life. In his martyrdom was his greatest triumph. A guilt-stricken nation mourned his death by forswearing violence. There was reason to hope that we had seen the last of communal strife and that India would indeed fulfill Gandhi's dream and become a Ram Rajya.

But that was not to be. Our hopes have turned to ashes. Hindu-Muslim confrontations on religious festivals have begun to occur with sickening regularity in riot-prone parts of the country where the two communities co-exist. From being Hindu versus Muslim, they have become Hindu versus Christian, Hindu versus Sikh, upper-caste Hindu versus lower-caste Hindu, Christian versus Buddhist, hill tribal versus plains' tribal. In the massacre at Nellie in Assam, it was just about everyone against his neighbour. It has become increasingly clearer that we are too many with not enough land or jobs available for all of us. The root cause of spreading endemic violence is economic : religious, linguistic and ethnic differences provide the excuse and motivation to indulge in it.

Poverty being the root-cause of violence, Bihar which is the poorest of the poor states of the union has never been able to free itself of it. If the poverty line is defined as an income of Rs.60/- (less than US $6) per month and a daily intake of 2000 calories, fifty-nine percent of Bihar, as compared to the national average of forty per cent, lives below the poverty line, writes Akbar. In this poverty-ridden state seven families comprise the feudal elite — all seven with formidable criminal records. including robbery, rape and arson. They maintain private armies, patronize dacoits, grab land belonging to poor and weak neighbours, win elections by rigging polls and using musclemen to crush opposition. And become ministers of government. The Marxist may well believe that property is theft, to the Bihari it is the other way round, theft is property.

Punjab does not fit into this neat summarization of poverty being the root-cause of violence because Punjab is the richest state of the Union and yet here 'violence leapfrogs'. The countryside appears prosperous and peaceful, but suddenly gunfire explodes and shatters its tranquillity. Fear spreads like a pall of venomous cloud and people reach for their guns. 'Punjab is', as the author points out, 'a lesson in how a few hundred terrorists armed with modern weapons, can hold people to ransom .... the lumpen and the religious extremists know they cannot take over the State, they have neither the armed strength nor the popular support for that; but they know how to create the environment in which they can thrive'. What made Sikhs of the Punjab turn fundamentalist and fanatic ? What made them elevate a demented hate-monger like Bhindranwale into a saint ? What made them kill innocent Hindus (and later innocent Sikhs) without any apparent purpose ? It would take many volumes to unravel the mystique of Bhindran- wale but the basic cause of its wide-spread acceptance amongst a section of the Sikh peasantry was economic — not poverty but the threat of impoverishment that hung over a people whose compara- tive prosperity had given them access to the good things of life. As long as the Green Revolution yielded a succession of bumper harvests and hundreds of thousands of their sons were able to go abroad to West Asia, England, Canada and the United States, they were able to ride on cloud nine. It was a life of transistor radios, audio-visual equipment, refrigerators, air-conditioners, motor-cycles and a *paooa* of country liquor at sundown. Then the yield from the land reached its optimum level, holdings of land came to be divided and sub-divided between sons and daughters of every generation; and foreign countries closed their doors to immi-grants. Where was the young farmer's son, who had finished school or college, to go to look for work ? There was not enough to do on the ancestral land; there was no industry in the State worth speaking of — not enough factories to process its cane, not enough flour and rice mills to process its wheat and rice, not enough textile mills to turn its cotton into cloth. The Central Government in its wisdom refused licenses to put up heavy industry because Punjab was uncomfortably close to Pakistan and therefore vulnerable. (Pakistan had no such inhibitions in setting up industries around Lahore, a bare 25 kilometers from the Indian border). The semi-educated, unemployed Sikh youth lent one ear to Bhindranwale's tirades against the Hindu Government in Delhi out to destroy the Sikhs and the other to Marxist-Naxalite propaganda. His aim could be either a separate Sikh State called Khalistan or the liquidation of the landed bourgeoisie. The means to both ends were common — the gun.

A class apart from both the poor Bihari and the comparatively affluent Punjabi, is that of the tribal. These once proud owners of large forests, have been reduced to servitude. Akbar compares their lot to those of flies caught in a spider's web. 'The threads by which the tribal has been trapped have taken a long time to weave. To create a good slave you must first kill his pride, his self-respect, his notion of himself as an ordinary, equal human being. The slave's body is needed — the man's for labour, the woman's for labour and abuse; but to control the body, the inner spark which ignites anger must be crushed. There are many weapons in the spider's arsenal, both psychological and physical, but the chief one is dramatically simple : hunger. When a generation or two dies of the ultimate denial, delirious for a handful of rice, while a chorus of spiders fattens indifferently in the background, physical and men-tal slavery becomes an easy option to the dying. The young woman at your feet is not prostrate through love or devotion; she is there because over many lifetimes she has learnt that the degradation of the spirit is the only guarantee she has against the degradation of the body, that food and safety are not her right but a gift which a superior may grant if she behaves.'

Indians often sanctimoniously describe themselves as spiritual people — by this token they feel they are somewhat superior to materialistic Westerners. It is true that Indians spend more time in prayer, religious ritual, pilgrimage and meditation than any other people in the world. But they are also the most money-minded and the quickest to draw their swords in the name of religion. 'More people have died in the defence of belief than truth,' writes Akbar of his countrymen. 'Men will gladly offer their blood, because heroes and martyrs, spurred by conviction, conquer nations in the name of superiority, and raise murder to a virtue in the defence of a piece of cloth. Those in power know this, and this is perhaps why they are in power. And of all the ideas that have either inspired men to achievement, or driven them to suicide, none has been more glorious or more dangerous than the concept of God. It is perhaps our ultimate conceit that we need to defend our version of Him, or that He cannot survive the decay of an institution in His name'. This, as should be obvious, is about the dispute over the Babari Masjid—Ram Janmabhumi temple at Ayodhya. He continues, 'The communalists had only one really good weapon : fear. Fear was the bow, and a whisper was the arrow. They told the Muslims that Hinduism would destroy their mosques, their laws, their ways of life, by the sheer weight of numbers and the help of a partial administration. They told the Hindus that Muslims were foreigners who would always kill and oppress, whose loyalty to this land would ever be doubtful. And every potential point of friction was seized and sharpened.'

*

M.J. Akbar's essays deal with incidents of mass violence that took place over the last six years and received wide publicity at the time they occurred. But very few reporters took the trouble of going to the remote villages where gunmen wiped out whole families in inter-caste warfare, or the place where a gangster's moll who was subjected to gang-rape and humiliation by a rival gang wreaked terrible vengeance by gunning down 20 men of the village where she had been dishonoured. This Akbar did. And much more. He visited towns like Jamshedpur, Mora'dabad and Meerut, Patiala, Batala and many others where Hindu-Muslim or Hindu-Sikh riots had taken place and found out what had triggered them off. Why, for instance, Hindu personnel of the Provincial Armed Constabulary (PAC) had gunned down upwards of seventy unarmed Muslims rounded up from villages near Meerut, an incident which earned strictures against the U.P.Government from Amnesty International. He spent days and nights among tribals and gained first-hand information about the cruel exploitation visited on them. He also travelled extensively to cover areas — like Darjeeling, Kurseong and Kalimpong which have become centres of the Gorkha agitation for a Gorkhaland — where violence is likely to erupt in the foreseeable future.

Akbar's first book, *The Siege Within* (Penguin) was a runaway success which quickly went into several editions. He was already acknowledged as much the most promising of India's young journalists, amongst the youngest editors of prestigious journals like *Sunday*. He capped his journalistic achievements by becoming the Editor-in-Chief of a major English newspaper, *The Telegraph*. The publication of *The Siege Within* established him as an author with rare insight into Indian politics, history and social problems. He writes with extraordinary skill and a felicitous turn of phrase. Reading him is sheer delight.

New Delhi   **KHUSHWANT SINGH**
January 1988

A Split-level War in Jamshedpur

The steel city of Jamshedpur has witnessed communal strife ever since the first steel mill was built. It is now a nouveau riche city with different communities competing for as much of the trade and commerce as they can. Wealth breeds crime as well as prosperity; the city has its share of the underworld. Tension has many causes, many faces. Religious festivals and processions lead to rioting which politicials are quick to exploit to their own advantage. Early in April 1979, Bala Saheb Deoras, head of the Rashtriya Swayam- sevak Sangh (RSS), a Hindu fundamentalist organization, visited Jameshedpur and exhorted Hindus to assert their rights in a Hindu country. Ten days later the city went up in flames, reducing entire localities to ashes and leaving scores of innocent men, women and children dead.

The city of Jamshet's* dreams has developed some ugly warts. It is an adolescent city, immature, vigorous, energetic, even rich; it wears fancy clothes and uses a good deal of cosmetics; but a disease has entered its lungs and heart, and its face breaks out in a hideous rash every now and then. Cosmetics and ugliness; the first does not hide the second, they exist side by side, in amazing complacence. The contrasts are startling. You see young engineers with their beautiful wives, the women laughing at some private joke as they motor home in the late afternoon, perhaps after lunch and tennis at the club. But ,in the city, down a broad, paved road lined with trees, fanned by cool breezes from the hills of Chotanagpur, is the posh and antiseptic Tata Medical Hospital where the more fortu- nate of the victims of communal violence are suffering, the sores now bandaged, but the wounds of the heart festering, and hate oozing from the eyes like a malignant pus that will contaminate all

*Jamshetji Tata, the founder of the House of Tatas.

that it touches. The rose garden of the Jubilee Park is a square of red on flowing green; charming, very charming, so soothing that you could sleep forever on the grass; why, so pretty that even Bombay film producers use it as a venue for songs that echo into the blue hills as macho hero and pneumatic heroine race into each other's arms and cling hard till the camera pans to two flowers making love. But the perfume is overwhelmed by the stench of the burnt, mutilated, shot, wounded, dying, dead, men, women and children at the Government hospital. The walls of this hospital are splashed with the black soot of age and carelessness;the atmosphere is septic, and the stench wafts out and onto the road, the nurses work hard for little reward, and on a bed sits a man injured in the head and leg, staring into space; beside him is his mother, also staring into space. Their world has burnt down. In the recesses of the hospital lie the dead, in hideous shapes, and each of them, each man, woman and child, has written a will in the presence of a hundred witnesses, and the will says that each member of the dead person's family receives a legacy of hate, an equal share each; and this legacy has no limits, no boundaries, so each member of the deceased may take what he or she can carry away.

Have you ever heard the silence of a city? Curfew time is five o' clock but long before that the silence has been building up. The city stopped roaring on 11 April 1979, but now as the sun enters the last quarter of its daily journey even the half-raised voices of the morning have hushed. The daylight is strong still. A cat drops quickly from a parapet onto Masjid Road and the eye, in reflex, catches the soundless movement for nothing else stirs, nothing else moves, there is no one on the street. Our car moves on, a window quickly shuts, soundlessly. Even the huge, squat, serried factory structures that fill the skyline of Jamshedpur seem afraid of making any noise. Dogs, scampering in the rubble of destruction, do not bark so much as whimper. The one sound that follows us is of the police; they are present at each street corner, neat and deadly guns in their hands, each picket with a plainclothes magistrate, and each picket stopping our car to check our curfew passes : the bold "Press" signs taped on the car are not sufficient proof of our innocence, and rightly so : stranger things are happening here than gun-running by fake journalists. A Muslim was nabbed carrying weapons in a Marwari's car; traders have no religion, as we have all heard, particularly traders in illegal arms. Chickens, owned by nobody now, are wandering about busily in deserted, broken, burnt and looted homes. Jagged bricks pockmark both sides of the road, bricks which are witnesses, weapons and finally victims of battle. A single slipper lies in the middle of the street. A lone cyclist, a Sikh, passes us, stares at us; he is on his way from work. The street lights are on; they have been on for the last few days as no one, in fear, has gone to switch them off; they become a little more noticeable in the gradually weakening sunlight, as dusk seeps towards this silent city. From the boundary walls of Agrico factory, Rajesh Khanna and Rekha promise Prem Bandhan. A bunch of crows sits on a speedbreaker; as our car nears, the crows trot off together, literally trot off. Now to less deserted streets; or seemingly less deserted — the shops and signs on either side make this street less forlorn. But in the shadows there is movement; beggars, without a home, stuck against the drawn shutters of the shops, wearing black rags, staring at the empty roads. Beggars and guardians of the law and a handful of journalists; that is all that moves in a curfew.

There is curfew too in the narrower lanes of Jugsalai, the business centre of the city, but here there are signs of life. This is where the merchants live and earn, and they are spending these unproductive evenings chatting on the verandahs, looking at the streets. It is getting dark now, and our car winds through lanes and bylanes in search of mood and battlefields. At one turn a loud 'Halt' stops us abruptly. Police scamper down from a rooftop. We are on the border of a Muslim area. The officer of the law is sceptical about our verbal assurances. He demands to see our curfew passes, and is not totally convinced by them. S. P. Singh, the editor of *Ravivar* is in our car. The policeman looks hard at S. P. Singh who wears a beard; 'Are you S. P. Singh?' he asks, and his voice has disbelief in every syllable. The editor of *Ravivar* has to show his identity card with his photograph to prove his point, and then the policeman almost reluctantly gives us back our curfew passes. We are two Muslims and two Hindus (purely by chance) in the car, and the two Hindus both wear beards that would do a Muslim proud. The picket thinks we are carrying arms for the Muslims. And in case we have any doubt that their attentions are only routine, one of them calls out as we depart: 'I hope there is nothing lethal in the boot'.

Law and order have two enemies: the Full Truth and the Complete Lie. When people realize the truth, they start revolutions. When they are fed lies they begin meaningless riots. Lies are the staple of every communal disturbance. They are spread by people who have a stake in this stupid violence, who have something to gain out of impoverished Hindus and Muslims fighting each other. Businessmen, traders, politicians, *goondas*, leaders of 'cultural organizations' (like the Hindu Rashtriya Swayamsevak Sangh — RSS) feed the people with lies, watch these lies become convictions in people's hearts, watch the passions build up, and then these leaders actually set up the events which will provoke a conflagration. They simply stick a pin into the nerves of people, and it is only a matter of time before the people explode. Then, when the first round of violence is over, when the initial steam has been let off, the lies keep on circulating. The people must not realize that they have been fooled or they will tear down their false heroes. There is fuel already in the murky events that make up communal violence, and upon this more lies are heaped and spread. After all, if the Hindu and Muslim live in peace, how will the RSS find another convert? How will the trader sell arms? How will a shopkeeper have the pleasure of seeing a rival's shop burn down? How will the *goonda* loot? How will the communalist kill a fellow human being? Keep the lies floating friends!

*

Item; a young man is escorting us out of Dimnabasti, the Adivasi (tribal) locality where the trouble had its physical origins. He is in his late teems and is visiting his brother on a holiday. He works in a transport company in Ranchi, and has a watch on his hand to prove his earning capacity. As we are leaving he asks us; 'How badly have the Adivasis been attacked in Delhi?' We assure him that there are no riots in Delhi. He says that someone has heard a report over the radio!

Item; Ganesh Sau, who is not an Adivasi, is chatting with a group of young Adivasi villagers. We want to talk to the villagers, but he begins answering on their behalf, and they recognize his leadership. He does not make clear what precisely he is doing there; he does not live there, he accepts. He says he has been 'working' in Dimnabasti for years. In the course of the conversation he tells up that the administration banned the *jhanda* (flag) procession despite a High Court order to allow it. This is not true, but Sau has apparently been led to believe it, and in turn the Adivasis of the village believe it and are worked up about it.

Item; on the Ranchi road, a few hundred yards away from Azadnagar, where the violence broke out, we discuss the riots with a group of young Hindu men. One of them, who despite his slightly ragged *dhoti* reads magazines and newspapers and keeps in touch with politics, insists; 'Muslims were using bullets made in America, China, Pakistan. Pakistani guns have been discovered. Please note, there are American arms. So you know who is behind these riots, who is arming the Muslims' We try and argue, but he will not be moved.

Item: A man sitting on his haunches in the cool of a shopfront in Daiguttu, speaks about the huge arsenal built up by the Muslims. 'The police have not seized anything from them' he says, 'I have been shot by foreign bullets.' This surprises us; foreign bullets would hardly allow a man to walk about freely. We ask him to show us the wounds. They are black pockmarks: the marks left by the charra (pellets) of countrymade guns, not by sophisticated bullets. When we point out the discrepancy, he smiles.

Item: Just opposite Azadnagar mosque we stop to take pictures. An angry young man, perhaps mistaking us for politicians, shouts, '*Sab kuch ho gaya to murdaghat pay aaye hain!*' (After everything is over they have come to the graveyard!) Fair enough. We begin talking to a person who looks a devout Muslim. He has a large handkerchief over his head; the mustache on his upper lip is cropped according to Islamic norm, his beard is full. He does not need much encouragement to begin his tale of woe. 'You should see the number of Muslim huts which have been burnt there,' he says, pointing across the field. 'One hundred, at least.' The actual damage is far less.

The misfortune is that lies are believed, and they generate the most dangerous of passions, the desire for revenge. It was to douse such passions that the authorities, perhaps for the first time in the

long history of communal riots in our country, released details of
how many Hindus and Muslims were killed and injured. And
perhaps this is why the authorities did not try too hard to artifi-
cially deflate the number of casualties. The figures tell a certain
story : both Hindus and Muslims suffered, though the latter
suffered much more, particularly in loss of homes and property.

*

During Bakrid, the Muslim festival, the knives come out for the
sacrifice of animals, and the police go on alert, as many Muslims
sacrifice cows. The gaiety of Holi,the Hindu spring festival, is
sometimes marred by tension when some stupid Muslims begin to
take objection to colour being sprayed on them. Moharrum sees
pseudo-martial Muslims taking out huge processions, carrying
weapons they have no business to have in the first place: it is an
aggressive display which has very little to do with the origins of this
sad day (Moharrum is the month of mourning in the memory of
Hassan and Husain) in the Islamic calendar. And now Ramnavami must be added to the list of 'sensitive ' festivals. Ramnavami
is the equally absurd Hindu answer to Moharrum. The flag of
Mahavir, the Lord Hanuman, is raised, and processions are taken
out where martial arts are displayed: it is a symbol of militancy,
and each procession contains the germs of communal violence. In
Jamshedpur today, as many as 72 *akharas* (processions) are taken
out every years.

*

On the outskirts of Jamshedpur is a colony of Adivasis. Dimnabasti. All the land of Jamshedpur once belonged to the Adivasis,
but now of course a hundred different people have acquired the
Adivasi land. Over ten years ago, a group of Muslims set up
Sabirnagar about two hundred yards away from Dimnabasti: the
intervening stretch of beautiful rolling fields is characteristic of the
Chotanagpur plateau. Two roads mark the boundaries of Sabirnagar: Road no.14 and Road no.15. They are not far apart; it is a
very small colony of mud huts. The roads are hardly roads; they
are mud tracks. While Road no.15 goes up to Dimnabasti, Road

no.14 stops short on this side of the fields separating the Adivasis from the Muslims. On Road no.14 is a thatched mosque which the Muslims have constructed; and there is a *madrasa* (Muslim religious school) on the premises of the mosque.

The immediate, though not the real, cause of the Jamshedpur riots was absurdly silly, but then that is in pattern too. How many lives have been lost over a loud drum or a mischievous prank! The processionists of Dimnabasti wanted to take their *jhanda* through Road no.14; the Muslims felt that they should go through Road no.15. The difference in the two routes was a matter of a few hundred yards. To go through Road no.14, the *jhanda* would have had to cut diagonally across the field, and then pass through a hundred yards of Muslim *basti*. On the way would fall the mosque. The Muslims pointed out that if the *jhanda* took Road no.15 straight to the main road, it would avoid the mosque too.

The Hindus refused to budge from their point of view. The road was a public thoroughfare, they insisted, and nobody could divert a procession of their's . The *jhanda* from Dimnabasti had begun only in 1978, and the previous year there had been trouble over the route, but the administration had not allowed the use of Road no.14. The matter went up to the High Court. The Court ruled that while Road no.14 was a public thoroughfare, it was up to the district administration to decide to give permission or not to the procession. The administration said this year, as it had said the previous year, that it would not allow the *jhanda* to go through Road no.14 and the War of the Egos started. Hindus and Muslims in Jamshedpur who had never set eyes on Road no.14 and 15 become experts on the subject. The Hindu point of view was simplified to this: How could the Muslims prevent them from taking out a legitimate Ramnavami procession? After all, Hindus never stopped Muslims from taking out their Moharrum processions. The Muslims said that the Hindus were deliberately establishing a right of way where none had existed before and this 'ridiculous' route, once established, would be an annual insult to the pride of the Muslims.

It was readily apparent that both sides were spoiling for a fight. Jamshedpur is the communalists' dream city for a hundred different reasons. There are the memories of 1964, when the Muslims were butchered by Hindus excited by tales of true and imagined torture of the Hindus of East Pakistan. Then too Adivasis were fed lies and used by Hindu leaders against the Muslims — the Adivasis were told that their brethren were being murdered in East Pakistan. This time, the Adivasis could add one more grievance to their short list of resentments against the Muslims (the two communities first fought each other only in 1964, and this is one of the saddest aspects of this nasty business — the Adivasis have been dragged into the communal war by elements of the RSS). After 1964, the few Muslims living in Adivasi majority areas decided to move out: Sabirnagar was the result of such reaction. Moreover, the Adivasis, who had watched for generations their land being either looted or bought at dirt cheap prices by everyone, starting from industrialists like the Tatas to every new community that settled down in Jamshedpur; the Adivasis who were still condemned by our society to live in ignorance and waste, whose women were still considered such easy game that there were no really established whore houses in the city, these Adivasis now found that even Muslims were buying land from them. Sabirnagar must have been a needle in the eye of the Adivasis living within sight. The Jamshedpur-Ranchi industrial belt is volatile for various reasons: urban pressures, the wealth generated by a fully-employed population, the fact that the city has no tradition (only one generation can really claim to have been born and brought up in the city.) The city of Jamshedpur itself has been a boiling pot of disparate fortune seekers from the inevitable Marwaris to the refugees from the Punjab who were promised a house and a future in the Fifties. There is the clash of temperaments and greed; moreover, the strong lumpen proletariat and *goonda* element make this city a haven for the mischievous.

Goondas have always been important leaders of such cities. The boomtown syndrome creates a strong underworld which steals and smuggles and brews cheap liquor and provides protection. Dhanbad of course is the classic example but Jamshedpur is not too far behind. The Thakurs control the Hindu underworld and they are adequately supported by the Marwaris. The Muslims too have their criminals, petty and not so petty, with colourful pseudonyms culled from the Hindi cinema. Recently, two important *goondas* died in Jamshedpur. The Hindus lost a godfather called Pyara Singh and the Muslims lost their Robin Hood, Anwar.

Pyara, after a long and lucrative career in crime, died a peaceful death. And Anwar, nicknamed Sikandar (after Alexander the great, no less) was killed in a police encounter. Both communities felt orphaned by the loss of these leaders; the Muslims, in particular, because Anwar was their sole superstar in the underworld. The Muslims felt so bad after the death of Anwar that they wanted to give him a hero's burial. The police very sensibly refused to allow any such nonsense. But it is a fact that both communities held the two godfathers in great esteem. The Muslims were grateful to Anwar; he had given them protection in the 1971 riots which means, of course, that the supplied them with arms. And, as one Hindu, a waiter in a restaurant, told us; 'If Pyara Singh were alive, there would not have been a communal riot.' Such is the faith of innocents. It is balderdash to say that the death of these two led to the riots, but it did nothing to reduce the tensions. With their protectors dead, the leaderless felt an increased panic and this must have been reflected in some of their subsequent decisions.

There is also the interesting, and important point that the Muslims of the city form one of the richest Muslim communities in the country. They have jobs; more than half the employees of Tisco, for instance, are Muslims. Muslims have also entered trade, while some Muslim *goondas* have had a profitable role to play in the illicit liquor business and money lending rackets. Muslims with any economic stake are the first targets of Hindu communalists. The Hindus are usually backed by business interests who want to displace the Muslims after they have been either economically destroyed or thoroughly demoralized. The history of riots shows clear efforts by landlords or traders to use the conflagration as a camouflage to do what they couldn't have achieved legally. Indeed, this is one of the principal reasons why businessmen feed communalists.

There are so many strands, and they are so tangled, that it is virtually impossible to disentangle them all and describe them . But the vital reason which provoked the Jamshedpur riots was caste and local politics (in Bihar, caste and politics are never too far from each other). After the Janata victory in March 1977, law and order in the north virtually collapsed, particularly in the industrial belt as the lameduck Congress ministry lost interest in ruling.

Things did not improve much with the coming of the Janata
Government in the State, but soon the Karpoori Thakur ministry
began finding its feet. By 1978, it was ready to take strong administrative decisions, and by the middle of that year, the complexion of
the administration in the region had altered. Dr Kumar Suresh
Singh, a scholar who had done his thesis on Adivasis, and a man
with an extremely good reputation as an officer, was lifted from
the comparative obscurity of the directorship of the Anthropolog-
ical Survey of India and made Commissioner of Singbhum. B. K.
Sinha became the Deputy Commissioner, the youthful U. K.
Singh came in as Sub Divisional Officer, and a Harijan, Ram
Swaroop, was made Superintendent of Police. It is a tribute to
these officers that whoever has gone to inquire into the riots at
Jamshedpur cannot question their integrity.

But the local mafia (and here we include the politicians)
obviously did not find these new officers very palatable. To begin
with they were honest: and honest officers can change the whole
chemistry of a corrupt city. The SP, particularly, is a vital figure;
and he refused to play the little games which the politicians and the
local mafia indulge in to display their power and control over the
administration. Among the people ignored by the SP was the local
Janata MLA, Dinanath Pandey, who has an RSS background,
and who played a key role in engineering the riots. According to
one source, the Janata politicians, working with the RSS and
others, including probably the Muslim Jaamat-e-Islami (the
organization which has been and continues to be the biggest enemy
of Indian Muslims), had decided to provoke communal riots as
early as October 1978. Their aim: to discredit the present administration and have the officers transferred. (I would like to stress that
the person who told us this was not a Government officer but a
local politicians.)

By the end of March 1979, everyone in Jamshedpur knew that a
communal riot was in the offing. A Janata leader in Patna even
warned the State Government about the impending crisis. In fact,
the one major criticism against the district administration is that
they could have taken stronger pre-emptive action to stop the riot.
In any case, by the end of March both communities had begun
stockpiling their weapons of offence and defence.

When Balasaheb Deoras, chief of the RSS, came to visit Jamshedpur on 1 April, talk of the Ramnavami procession was already polluting the air. Among other things, Mr Deoras told this faithful audience that it was very sad that in their own country Hindus were not allowed to take out their religious processions. He also pointed out that though the number of mosques was increasing in India, no Muslim country allowed a Hindu temple to be constructed. It is pointless to comment further on such statements: they tell their own story. The RSS is not so much an organization (cultural or political, take your pick) as a state of mind. It is the physical form given to an attitude towards the minorities, particularly the Muslims. It represents Hindu revivalism of the worst sort; in its heart it is still taking revenge against Aurangzeb, the Mughal Emperor. Its influence on the Hindu community varies with time and place but during communal tension its impact is wide, and RSS members become the most dangerous clandestine force, determined to provoke violence. Naturally, they do not admit this publicly. Publicly, there is sweetness and light, hobnobbing with the Jamaat-e-Islami. This friendship should not surprise anyone. After all, the Jamaat is a communal body itself, and since both draw sustenance from communalism, they could often be working together to arouse tension. Mr Deoras, in Jamshedpur, for instance, received a pen from the local Jamaat leader, Shamim Ahmed Madni. It was a gift of friendship, and the pen was significant as Mr Madni had brought it from the holy country of Saudi Arabia.

By 5 April, the administration had refused permission for the use of Road no.14. On the previous night, efforts had been made by Hindu and Muslim leaders, including the local MLAs (Jamshedpur also has a Muslim Janata MLA, Mohammed Ayub) to effect a compromise, but no agreement was reached. Some processions were begun, but stopped by Hindus who insisted that until the Dimnabasti dispute was settled, Ramnavami would not be celebrated. The Muslims, also, were being instigated by communalists among them, but they kept a low public profile. In protest against the administration, the Hindus forced closures of shops and cinema halls.

The administration made arrests, while the leaders continued to argue and debate over a compromise. On 7 April, the Sri Ramnavami Kendriya Akhara Samiti issued a pamphlet which cannot be called anything but utterly communal in character: indeed rarely do the instigators of riots display their hand so openly.

This pamphlet was headlined 'An appeal to the Religion-loving Public of Jamshedpur.' Two shoulder headlines said, *Dharma ki jai ho* and *Adharma ka naash ho* (Victory to religion and Destroy those who do not believe). The appeal said: Till now the people have borne every cruelty peacefully, but in the name of peace the Hindus of this area are being crushed. In Dhakidih, the police destroyed an image of the Lord Hanuman, in Jugsalai the police rained lathis and tear gas; in Mango, the Hindus have been reduced to a minority. It is clear that behind this are the SP and some sycophantic officers of his. What is clear is that all the constables, havildars, Home Guards, etc., are ready to support us...The reasons why you could not take out your processions on the *dashami* remain, and as long as this corrupt and anti-Hindu SP stays here, images will continue to be destroyed. But in this struggle we must remember our culture and our self-respect. Keeping this in mind, the Sri Ramnavami Akhara Kendriya Samiti has decided that all the *akharas* will come out at two in the afternoon on Wednesday, 11 April, which is Hanuman Jayanti. Only the Mango (that is the Dimnabasti) *akhara* will come out at eleven in the morning, and pass through Road no.14. According to our decision, everyone will come here first, bring out this *akhara*, and then disperse to their localities to bring out their processions...We want to tell the Governor of Bihar, the Chief Minister, the district officials and all the policemen and officials that if any untoward incident takes place during these peaceful processions then the full responsibility for that rests on the shoulders of the administration. So, the administration must make arrangements for safety with impartiality.

Declarations of war have been more polite. This was open provocation and it sent the temperature of the city higher than ever. (One hopes that the people who see no RSS involvement in communal riots will take notice of such pamphlets.) Efforts continued to be made by some sane men to prevent the coming bloodshed, but the leaders of the Hindus were adamant. Eventually a compromise was reached: the procession would begin on Road no. 15 and turn into Road no.14 through a connecting mud track. It was also decided that some Muslims would accompany the procession to see it through safely.

Meanwhile, in response to the call Hindus began assembling at Dimnabasti early on the morning of the 11th carrying weapons in their hands, officially for the games. At eight in the morning the *jhanda* left Dimnabasti. Only about twenty-five people from Dimnabasti itself accompanied the *akhara*; the rest were outsiders. The procession went through the designated route, and with a lot of noise but no violence reached the main road. In fact there was virtually no damage in the Dimnabasti-Sabirnagar area, apart from a couple of burnt huts (no one was injured). When we saw the two colonies they looked angelically peaceful. Commenting on this, a police officer standing guard told us with a laugh: *Yahan to Bajrangbali khud baithe they — poonch ghuma ke chale gaye, Lanka jaltee rahi* (Bajrangbali himself was sitting here; he turned and went away and left Lanka burning).

There was a sigh of relief as the procession reached the main road; but the sigh was premature. The next point where trouble could arise was in Mango, less than a kilometre down the road, where the procession would go through a Muslim area. The procession progressed very slowly. This was clearly an effort to delay the procession till eleven o'clock, when Hindus from all over the city were scheduled to join the procession as per the pamphlet. The number of processionists kept growing: there were at least 15,000 people in it now. In the lanes of Mango, particularly in Azadbasti and Azadnagar, the Muslims began gathering, some afraid of the violent mood of the processionists, and some with mischief on their minds. Both sides were prepared for battle: the tension had taken its toll on the nerves.

A little after ten, the procession stopped opposite the mosque which stands on the main road. The administration was eager that the procession move quickly from there; if this point could be crossed peacefully there was every chance that the riots might have been averted. But it was at this sensitive point that the Janata MLA and old Jana Sangh hand, Dinanath Pandey, played his trump card to ensure that the riots did take place. He announced that the procession would not move until the administration released all the Hindus who had been arrested earlier! The Commissioner and other officials pleaded that even if they wanted to they could not do this: they could not release the prisoners without any legal proceedings. But Mr Pandey in his wisdom would not be budged. Inflammatory speeches were made. As V.N.Mishra, a magistrate who was on duty all through, and had had little sleep the previous night, put it: 'We thought around eleven that the danger was almost over and in an hour's time I could have a bath and catch up on some sleep. But as it happened I could only snatch a few biscuits to eat during the next 24 hours.'

At 11-40 a.m. the inevitable happened. A stone was thrown. A bomb exploded. The rest was murder.

The Muslims of Mango were prepared for the violence; they had obviously been instigated by their communalists (there is hardly any shortage of this breed among the Muslims), and they held their own in the ensuing battle. They also attacked the Hindu areas of Daiguttu, until they were repulsed by the police. The Muslims were the aggressors here. Anil Prasad Srivastava, a Tata apprentice died, the parents of a child called Kailash were butchered; A temple was attacked. Arrows and guns were freely used (by both sides), and the mute evidence of the battle was to be seen in arrows stuck on lampposts or on the top of huts, in jagged bullet marks on walls and most of all in the eyes of parents who had lost children, on the faces of women who had lost their homes.

At the same time as the Muslim attacks all over Jamshedpur, as if on cue, mobs of Hindus began attacking Muslim areas. And this time the police, instead of defending those who here being attacked, joined the mobs and looted and destroyed Muslim homes. The Bihar Military Police, packed with caste Hindus from Arrah, Ballia and Chapra, wrote their names in the history of shame. The pamphleteers were not wrong, apparently, when they said that the constables and the havildars were on their side. They would help smash open closed Muslim doors with the familiar abuse on their lips: *Saala, yahan Pakistan bana raha hai*! (*Saala*, you are making a Pakistan here!) They were not a peace-keeping force, they became the armed wing of the RSS. Only the Gorkhas of Company One behaved with any impartiality; the rest went berserk.

Once again, it was the senior administration that tried to inject some order and sense. But the criminal failure of the police is evident from the speed with which the Army was called out. The Army began patrolling around six in the evening; by eleven at night it had received its formal orders to enforce law and order. And immediately they made an impact. The Indian Army remains one of our proudest achievements, and the sheer faith that the people have in it speaks volumes for its role in our society. Everywhere it was the Army (and the soldiers and officers came from all communities) which displayed the impartiality and strength that prevented much greater damage. It is impossible to praise the Army enough. Sadly, the communalists know this too. And in order to discredit the armed forces, at least two bands of *goondas* disguised themselves in Army uniforms in order to continue the havoc (they were arrested later). This indicates, too, how planned the whole business was.

The riots took place in three stages. First, came arson; then, stabbings plus arson; last came the evacuation to refugee camps. And perhaps the saddest incident in this tragedy took place during the evacuation of an ambulance load of refugees: this was reminiscent of the trains to Pakistan and India during the horrible Partition riots. After twelve hours of violence on 11 April, some time after one at night, the administration was able to arrange for vehicles to pick up Muslims surrounded in the school and the mosque in Bhalubasa. The Army had been called out, and had begun restoring order. Tata Medical Hospital's ambulances, buses, trucks, and sundry other vehicles were pressed into service. Ambulance number BRX 6112 was part of the second convoy, and was carrying about sixty people (estimates vary, but this is probably the most reasonable figure). It was being driven by an Adivasi and was in the middle of the convoy, which was being escorted at the head and at the back by police jeeps. Two police guards were actually inside the ambulance, in order to provide protection in case of any mishap.

As the convey was crossing a bridge over Kharkai river, in the Kashidih *mohalla*, this ambulance suddenly veered off into a side lane. None of the vehicles following bothered to stop and check. The driver immediately behind later said that he thought it was part of the ambulance's planned route. The police vehicles also did not bother to investigate.

The ambulance was driven a short distance into the lane and the driver and the policemen decamped. On cue, a mob attacked the ambulance and set fire to it. The Commissioner was a little behind the convoy. When he reached the lane he saw the ambulance burning, and heard the cries for help of the women and children trapped inside, burning to death.

He charged towards the ambulance but most of the damage had been done. He could save only a handful, and they too had severe burns. The rest of the people inside were dead. In a similar crime, a bus with six Muslims was burnt: all died.

*

'I cannot comprehend this...it is alien to my way of thinking...it is the worst experience of this nature in this steel city in my experience' said Rusi Mody, the managing director of Tata Iron and Steel Company (TISCO) — he was not in Jamshedpur during the 1964 riots. When we went to see him, the top executive of TISCO explained that he would have liked to call us home, but he was not in a position to offer even a reasonable cup of tea because of the shortage of essential items. The riots stopped trade (though not production at TISCO). Our photographer, Krishna Murari Kishan starved all through 12 April, when he reached Jamshedpur; finally he bought a potato for five rupees, boiled it and ate it. Even when we reached the city, on 16 April, hotels were refusing to take any guests: Raj Hans hotel generously reopened to accommodate us. And if things were bad for visitors like us, they were terrible for the poor residents of Jamshedpur — they went without food and water.

TISCO began relief work as soon as the refugee camps were set up, supplying 40,000 meals a day, and rushing in blood plasma from Calcutta. The Tata companies must receive the credit for good work, quickly done. The price that the city had to pay for this four-day madness was enormous. Nearly 1,600 pucca houses had to be completely rebuilt. But it is not the economic damage, great though it is (Muslims have inevitably suffered more), but the damage to community relations that remains immeasurable. People's faith has been wounded, how long it will take to repair it, God alone knows. Each memory will remain etched permanently on the minds of yet another generation, particularly the children, who were innocent on the morning of 11 April, but grew up suddenly during the hours of hate and violence. Children like Kailash, whose parents were butchered. One hundred and thirty eight houses were demolished in Bhalubasa. Harijan *bastis* were attacked by Muslims, Harijans attacked Muslims and damaged a Muslim graveyard. Adivasis let loose their deadly arrows. Slogans of revenge rent the air. There was passionate anger. There was betrayal. And not enough of trust and not enough of the generosity which Kadua witnessed when a Sikh, S.B.Singh, and a Muslim ,Maula Sahib, personally joined hands and prevented the two communities from going mad in their small area. The sadness and death and desolation after the riots is a memory that will endure We saw a charred cycle, two burnt babies' milk bottles, a bucket, a half-opened briefcase with a pair of pyjamas in it; the only thing which had survived intact was a model Taj Mahal in a glass case. Next door was the house of a man who obviously did some reading. A book, *Rajniti Shastra ke Mool*, lay on a shelf: the rest of the books had been burnt. On his door was stencilled the All India Tilak Hatao Committee. A framed picture showed a group at Ranchi College: this was the Bazme Adab of 1968-69, presumably the man who lived here was standing in that picture. And in another house a box had been ripped open and looted. What was left was the photograph of a child. Nobody seemed to have wanted to loot the photograph. If the child had survived how could he ever forget those hours in his life?

To make matters worse, even as the embers continued to flicker, the communalists returned to their game, their lust for blood undiminished. In the third week of April, a rumour swept the city that the Ramnavami procession would be taken out again as it was interrupted the last time, and the puja could not be completed! Any sane person could have seen this was madness but there was revenge and blood in the eyes of too many people. And the lies are still circulating. The history of communal riots shows that rarely has a riot ended after just one bout between the two communities.

In Daiguttu, Professor Zakee Anwar, a senior professor of the Karimia College, lived. In early April he had received an invitation from All India Radio to give a talk on national integration. Professor Anwar had also written a story on an Indian Muslim's love for his country in *Biswin Sadi*, an Urdu magazine. One day before the riots, he went on a fast in order to prevent them. On the morning of the riots, Professor Anwar shifted his family away, since he lived in a Hindu area and the rest of the Muslims of Daiguttu had decided to leave. Professor Anwar never left his house himself, as he could not believe anything could happen to a man of his secular principles.

In the afternoon, Professor Zakee Anwar was dead. Does our country have no place for people like Professor Anwar?

April 1979

Massacre in Moradabad

The population of Moradabad, famous for its brassware, divides almost equally between Hindus and Muslims. This was a recipe for peace rather than violence, at least generally. Then, suddenly, with the astonishing fury of a violent storm in a calm sky, came the morning of 13 August 1980. Men of the Provincial Armed Constabulary (PAC) opened fire on about 40,000 Muslims while they were at their Id prayers. No one knows exactly how many people died. What is known is that the incident at Moradabad was not a Hindu-Muslim riots but a calculated, cold-blooded massacre of Muslims by a rabidly communal police force which tried to cover up its genocide by making it out to be a Hindu-Muslim riot.

Moradabad was a case of police brutality, pure and simple. The forces of 'law and order' unleashed their fury on thousands of Muslims who had come to offer prayers on their day of joy and celebration; hundreds died, including many children, in the massacre and the stampede. And hundreds were injured; for many of them death came slowly. Both the Hindus and the Muslims of Moradabad are telling anyone who will listen that what happened on 13 August 1980 in their city was not a communal riot: it was a straight clash between the police and the Muslims. But the police, in order to throw a cover on their brutal misdeeds, told lies about what precisely happened, and built up false trails that would shift the focus of attention from the incidents of the *namaz*. Moradabad was not communal on 13 August but the police might have made it communal later.

After a long month of daylong fasting, during which not a morsel of food, not a drop of water may pass the gullet between first light and sunset, Muslims gather on their rooftops to search for that thin sliver of gold which will appear for ten minutes or so on the western sky as the sun melts into the horizon below it. This is the new moon which will announce the end of the month of Ramzan, and the beginning of the most joyous day in the Muslim calendar — the day of Id. This is the day which Muslims await: new clothes are made, presents are distributed, the sweet *sewai* is offered as a sign of friendship. The high point of Id is the *namaz*, to which Muslims go early in the morning, dressed in their new clothes, perhaps with a little attar in their ear. Apart from the adult women, everyone else goes to the Id prayers including all the children, both boys and girls. The *namaz* is a celebration of God's goodness, and a reaffirmation of brotherhood, a concept which finds expression in the gesture which has become synonymous with Id — the embrace.

More than 50,000 Muslims gathered at the Idgah (the name means where Id prayers are held) of Moradabad. Sixty per cent of this city of five lakh people is Muslim, and Id obviously is one of the major celebrations of the town. Buntings with *Id Mubarak* written on then flutter from shops; painted advertisements on walls encourage you to smoke Biri 788 in the first line, and wish you happiness on Id in the last. The Idgah is a largish open field, walled on the sides, with one entrance leading to the main road. At one corner of the Idgah, near the main road, is a small mosque called Ek Raat Wali Masjid, because it had been constructed decades ago in one night.

As usual the Muslims came for the prayers bedecked in their new clothes. They brought all their children along. (The desperate theorists, who have tried hard to unearth a deepseated, widespread Muslim conspiracy against the police, might like to consider this point: would Muslims who came to fight bring their small, innocent children along with them to get massacred?) As usual, the crowd spilled over from the Idgah onto the main road, on which the *namazis* spread pieces of cloth and formed the traditional rows for the prayers.

Just opposite the Idgah, across the main road, are shops owned by Punjabi Hindus, and nearby is a Punjabi colony. Various organizations had set up *shamianas* near these shops to offer Muslims Id greetings after the prayers. At every such gathering in the country, the local administration posts policemen to ensure that nothing untoward happens. Some of the force was posted at the *shamiana*; other policemen were on the main road at the point where the congregation which had spilled over onto the roads finally ended.

The *namaz* is divided into three clear sections. First, come the genuflections, which take a couple of minutes during the Id prayers. Then the congregation sits and hears the Imam recite passages from the Quran: this is the *khutba*, and takes about five minutes. The whole congregation then raises its hands in *dua*, which lasts a minute or two, and the *namaz* is over. It was during the *khutba* that a pig wandered into the *namaz*.

First question: did the pig actually wander into the *namaz*? We met eyewitnesses, including one who was not a Muslim, who confirm that it did. The dispute between the people praying and the policemen arose when the Muslims asked the policemen how the pig had wandered in despite the presence of the police. After all, prayers had been held at that Idgah for generations, and the Harijan colony which is nearby had also existed for as long as anyone cares to remember: so how come a pig, which is considered by Muslims to be an unclean animal, that would completely destroy the sanctity of the prayer, had never disturbed the *namaz* before, and only chose to do so that year - despite a police force being right there?

The policemen told the Muslims that it was not their job to prevent pigs from disturbing the *namaz*. Therefore, question number two. Was it the policemen's job to stop the pig or not? On the face of it, it would seem a silly reason for such havoc, but only those who have no idea about Muslim sentiment would expect Muslims not to get agitated if a pig disturbed their prayers - particularly if they thought that the police had deliberately sent the animal. A friend of mine, who is in politics, whose integrity I trust, and whose secularism I have faith in, commented: 'How can I make a statement asking the police to stop pigs from disturbing a *namaz*? Is that their job?' The only reply to that I can give is: supposing a bunch of communal Muslims took a cow in front of a temple while a huge crowd had gathered for prayers, and started to slaughter it, would it be the job of the police to stop this stupidity or not? A pig in a *namaz* is just as provocative, and every administration in the districts of Uttar Pradesh knows it. It is not a question of reason or rationale: this is simply how a community feels.

This altercation took place where the congregation was tapering off; and then suddenly everything began happening very quickly. Within the five minutes that it takes to read the *khutba* and complete the *dua* the police had opened fire. The *dua* was not complete before the deadly whine of bullets speeding through or into the massed *namazis* began. One person, who was at the prayers, described it thus: 'During the *khutba* I heard a noise from the back. People started standing up, trying to see what had happened. Then they sat down again. But before the *dua* was over, the noise of the quarrel became very loud, and then before anyone could really react we heard the sound of bullets.'

The Imam who was at the microphone saying the *dua* stopped, and began appealing to the police to stop this madness of firing into a throng of *namazis*. Nobody listened. The local Congress (I) MLA, Hafiz Mohammad Siddique, who was there also appealed over and over again to the police to stop. But they had gone berserk. A stampede began and cries of pain filled the air as terrified children came under the feet of the fleeing crowd. More and more bewildered people were hit by bullets.

The police have told many lies to cover up their criminal assault on a defenceless congregation but these lies fall to pieces under scrutiny. The first lie they tried to circulate was that they were fired upon by a Muslim, and that armed Muslims were sitting at the prayers waiting to create trouble. The police killed many that day: did they recover any arms from anyone in that congregation? The police say, very correctly, that a Senior Superintendent of Police (SSP) of their's was injured, and claim that five constables died and four are missing. True, the SSP was injured at the Idgah, but did any of the constables die at the Idgah? Or did they die much later, when an infuriated mob of Muslims decided to take revenge by attacking the police *chowki* (outpost) at Galshahid? The police also tried to create the impression that Muslims began brickbatting first and that they only opened fire in defence. Another lie. The police opened fire within less than five minutes of the altercation; the brickbatting came later. After the stampede had started outside the Idgah, Muslim youth who saw how the police were behaving,loosened the top layer of bricks from one of the walls surrounding the Idgah and started hurling them at the police. The real truth is that if the police,whatever the provocation, had simply waited another two minutes or so for the *namaz* to end, and people to get up, the carnage would never have taken place. But the police acted with communal fury.

Even as the violence became a confrontation, thousands of Muslims began fleeing whichever way they could. The fact that the Idgah was walled became a major disadvantage. There are some Muslim houses adjacent to one wall; from these windows women hurriedly threw down ladders and children were pulled up to the windows and brought to safety. Many rushed through the one exit which seemed safe — the mosque. But the police later actually entered the mosque and fired right on the courtyard of the mosque, according to eyewitnesses. Dr Naseem Ahmed recounts that he helped pick up twenty-four bodies from the compound of the mosque, including thirteen children.

The police undoubtedly caused havoc. Many Muslims who were killed cannot be traced: the police have no 'record' of the bodies. To give just one example: Salim Mohammad was twenty-five years old, and he had been married to young Naeema just five months earlier. He was a worker who polished brass in one of the factories which have made Moradabad famous all over the world. He went to the Idgah, which is hardly five minutes away from his house, to pray; he never returned. A friend of his who was sitting nearby saw a bullet hit the side of Salim's face. Salim fell dead. This friend went to the fallen Salim, removed the only thing of value he had, a wristwatch, and brought it back to the family. (We saw the watch when we met the family; it was a poor man's watch, a brand called Siwa: it had been given to Salim as a wedding present by his wife's family.) Today Salim's body cannot be traced. His family have asked for it, but the police say they cannot find a Salim among the dead.

It was after ten o'clock that an outraged mob of Muslims attacked the Galshahid police *chowki*, in violent reaction. As one Muslim put it, 'What did you expect the Muslims to do after having seen their children killed on Id? Throw flowers at policemen?' It was during this attack that policemen were killed by the mob, the *chowki* burnt, and two rifles stolen.

But it is this attack by the Muslims, more than anything else, which proves that the violence on that day was not at all communal in nature. On the way to the Galshahid police post, the mob could have attacked many Hindu houses, shops and factories: they did not. Right in front of the Ek Raat Wali Masjid, right in the heart of the violence, is, for instance, the New Kumar Brass-work factory. This is totally within the densely populated Muslim Idgah *mohalla*, and if the Muslims had wanted to ransack it nobody could have stopped them from doing so. When we visited this place on 15 August, Hindu workers were living on the premises of the factory, and the factory was still safe. We met Dharam Singh, one of those who was staying there, and he assured us that there had been no trouble this far.

If the mob which could reach a police outpost had wanted, it could have attacked the Punjabi Hindu colony just across the road from the Idgah; or it could have raided the large Harijan colony which is barely a couple of hundred yards away from the Muslim localities. But there was no attack on non-Muslims; the only target was the uniform—of the U.P police or the hated Provincial Armed Constabulary (PAC),which, time and again, has proved its notoriety. It cannot be repeated often enough that there was no communal riot in Moradabad. There was no RSS involved; and despite all the efforts of the police to call this a Muslim League or Razakar (member of the Majlis-e-Ittahadul Muslimeen which wanted Hyderabad to declare independence in 1947 and 1948) instigated riot, they have not succeeded in convincing too many people. It was simply a case of the force meant to preserve law and order becoming thoroughly irresponsible. As Shamsul Islam, general secretary of the city Congress (I) commented, 'There was no government.' Prime Minister Indira Gandhi herself admitted that the administration was in bad shape. She went on to blame the Janata and the Lok Dal Governments for this, but this is hardly the point. Similarly, the Opposition said the Congress (I)'s use of the police for political purposes accounted for the extraordinary arrogance of the police; but the argument is less important than the fact that we seem to be reaching a stage where policemen are becoming a law unto themselves, a force of petty dictators. The sheer contempt which the Moradabad police, for instance, showed for the local Congress (I) MLA was revealing. Who will dare police the police? The District Magistrate and the police officer in charge on Id day in Moradabad have been transferred promptly, but are such transfers any real solution?

On the 14th and 15th of March the police are alleged to have begun efforts to give the disturbances a communal colour, to shift attention from their misdeeds. The atmosphere in the city was volatile enough. The Muslims were livid with anger, and anger is fertile breeding ground for violence. And when there is anger,tension, there is fear, myths and impressions that have been buried in the subconscious begin to dance before one's eyes; and even yesterday's friend becomes suspect because he was born with a certain name. Communalists, of whom there is no shortage in our country, come to the fore to take over temporary leadership of enraged minds. Rumour is king. Creating communal trouble is not too difficult in such an atmosphere. The encouraging thing is that, by and large, both communities showed commendable restraint, given what could have happened.

Some journalists did not have even that to commend them and went along with police efforts to use 'respectable' media to transfer the lies to the rest of the country — thankfully there were just a few; the majority, by far, were above reproach. There was, for instance, the banner headline in one important national English paper which said that four Border Security Force (BSF) jawans had been killed, obviously by Muslims. The BSF not merely immediately denied the story, but took a special press party around to show that no one on its force had been injured in any way. This story came from, one presumes, the police, unless the correspondent literally made it up. Well, there was one story which was literally made up. A report appeared, again from a journalist who claimed to be sitting in Moradabad, that 500 armed Muslims had come from Sambhal and attacked the police headquarters. It so happened that we were at Moradabad on the 15th, the day on which this attack was said to have taken place, and everyone could see that nothing had happened to the *kotwali*. And yet this correspondent, filing a story from Moradabad, 'reported' the attack. Similarly, the police tried to give the impression that there were a great number of Hindu victims too, so that the impression would be created that a communal riot had taken place but that again was simply not true. Almost all the Moradabad victims were Muslims, who died or were injured during that terrible incident at the Idgah.

*

There is a saying in western UP that the people here have been blinded by greenness (*hariyali ke andhen hain*). This is rich and fertile agricultural country, quite different from the uncertain colours of central UP or the dust of eastern UP. This is, comparatively, a rich area, well irrigated, and the people have the confidence that comes from full stomachs.

There are large populations of Muslims who have been traditionally politically articulate, and whose support means the difference between victory and defeat to a political party.

Guns are hardly an unknown commodity. The gun is a status symbol, a weapon of defence against robbery, and a symbol of power among both Hindus and Muslims. When guns are available, they also tend to come out easily. This is what makes a communal disturbance in western UP so much more potentially murderous than anywhere else. A Hindu-Muslim conflagration here is dangerous in the extreme. And there are enough vested interests on all sides who stand to gain by it — the Muslim League, for instance, which, despite its strident provocations, has not been able to make sufficient headway, politically, among Muslims. Conversely, the Rashtriya Swayamsevak Sangh (RSS) or the Bharatiya Janata Party (BJP), stands to gain if the Hindu vote consolidates along communal rather than political lines.

The vultures that inhabit every community are only waiting for an incident like the one that happened at Moradabad to take place. This will be their source of sustenance for a long while. Time and distance destroy the truth of any event:embellishments will make the Moradabad clash into a weapon for all kinds of motivated forces. A communal incident is like a selfsustaining bomb made of plasticine; the bomb can be moulded into whichever shape you want, and it will prove equally deadly wherever it is placed. Organizations like the Jamaat-e-Islami have been provided enough ammunition by the police in Moradabad to incite Muslims. The PAC, which in the past has already been condemned by inquiry commissions for partisanship, now has given Muslims one more very good reason to distrust it.

It is easy to get depressed about Moradabad. But hidden behind the filth of the violence lie certain important truths about both the people of India and our institutions which more than restore the balance. The quiet but splendid job done by the BSF and the Army in restoring the confidence of the fear-stricken people, for instance. In riot after riot (and I have covered too many of them) one has seen the people wait for the Army or the BSF to rescue them, not only from their enemies among the civilians but also their enemies among the police.

But how often can you bring out the Army to do the job which the police should be doing? The immediate aftermath of the Moradabad riots was Muslim anger in a dozen towns; this was only to be expected-you cannot hope that Muslims will sit and watch calmly hundreds of *namazis* being killed. No, they will demonstrate, and ask the Government to punish the guilty. But there is always more than simply this where Muslims are concerned. History, Pakistan: the myth that has in the subconscious, the myth of the sword-wielding Mussulman, which at times even sends a quiver of doubt into the sanest non-Muslim and which prompts him to ask himself whether the Muslims are basically an unreliable, emotional, anti-national community? Why do they keep fighting all the time? An easy answer would be that the cry of the minority must always compete against the cacophony of vested interests which want to either suppress it or exploit it; and when myriad cries fill the air it is very difficult to sort out the truth from the confusion.

Indian society is a conglomeration of a lot of volatile groups competing for the diminishing rewards of a stagnant or shrinking economy. At certain periods, tensions which are dormant become dominant, lighting fires in hundreds of places. Not all the cities closed by curfew today are victims of communalism. But communalism remains perhaps the most serious threat to our existence and integrity. There are enough people, both Hindu and Muslim, who are anti-national, who would like to see the tremendous experiment called India, born out of the faith of a saint called Mahatma Gandhi, destroyed. The most heartening thing I found about Moradabad was that, despite the intense provocation, the Hindus and the Muslims of the city were not spitting hate at each other. More than sixty per cent of the city is Muslim, and the Muslims were angry; and the Muslims had enough communalists within them who would have liked to provoke the community to convert the riot into a Hindu-Muslim war. But that did not happen. It could have happened so very easily. Particularly when all kinds of rumours, including ones which said that mosques had been burnt, were being spread on the 14th and the 15th.

The Muslims of India have many enemies, quite a few of whom actually publicly rejoice in the fact of their enmity towards this community. But perhaps their greatest enemy lies among themselves. This enemy is, by and large, kept in check by the community itself. He is not supported during elections; he is not given too much social respect. But he is always there, waiting for the Muslim mind to be provoked; he is waiting for the day when the Muslims of a village, of a city, of a district, of a State, of the country, will reject their secular leadership and turn to him. He is waiting and dreaming for that day. I saw this enemy lurking in one *mohalla* of Moradabad. He was a resident of that *mohalla*. We went in to talk to the Muslims about what happened, and they began narrating their experiences, showing us the wounds on the bodies of their children, and on the hearts of the adults. Then this man walked in. He was large, bloated. His pyjamas stopped above the ankle. His thin regulation mustache drew a black line above the upper lip. He had small eyes that stared keenly at us: were they wondering why we do gooders' had come? Did our presence reduce one weapon in his arsenal? He sat there quietly, waiting, listening; watching. Waiting to be recognized by us as The Leader. Every muscle on his face, every dart from his eyes, said: my time has come.

He was the local leader of the Jammat-e-Islami.

Postscript: We were waiting in the bright afternoon sunlight outside the *kotwali* (police headquarters). The *kotwali* had become the fulcrum around which administration in Moradabad was revolving after the city sank into the fearful silence and tension of curfew at five pm, Wednesday, 13 August. A regular stream of vehicles carrying different kinds of authority —officials, politicians, policemen, Army — caused a strange traffic jam. A traffic jam looks so incongruous in a deserted city. Just opposite the *kotwali* was the only shop which was open in Moradabad a sweetmeats shop mainly servicing the police.

Suddenly a heavy police truck screeched to a halt. Out jumped four policeman, very brisk indeed, dragging behind them a man who was still bleeding from an open wound on the left side of his head. The blood was pouring down the side of his face, and had soaked parts of his shirt. His face was swollen; there was terror in

his eyes; he was shivering. Kamal Sahai, our photographer, immediately turned his camera towards the bleeding victim. The
policeman whose hand interfered with the picture suddenly
realized that a photograph was being taken, and rushed in front of
the camera. But by this time one picture, we thankfully found out
later, had been taken. We were brusquely told not to take any more
pictures. Why? Who was this man? We followed him into the
kotwali, but were prevented by the constables holding him from
talking to him. We appealed to a senior officer (who had been sent
to Moradabad on special duty). He was a very sophisticated,
soft-spoken officer, very unlike some of his arrogant and stupid
brethren on the police force. He finally relented and gave us
permission: a couple of minutes, and no pictures please.

The man's name was Shakeel Ahmad. He had been arrested for
breaking curfew, near the police canteen. He said that he to supply
milk regularly to the canteen, and was well-known there. After two
days (this was on the 15th), he had become bored of sitting at home
and had gone to eat a *paan* in the police lines and was returning
home along with a friend called Babu Singh when he was nabbed
by the police. They asked the two their names, told Babu Singh to
push off, put Shakeel in the van, and beat him up badly before
bringing him to the police station.

And then one of the policemen who had brought him in, and
who was listening to our conversation, could not control himself
any more. He first abused Shakeel Ahmad, then turned to us and
said, 'This chap had gone to the police lines to collect information
about the police which he could pass on to the Muslims.'

Nobody tried to deny that Ahmad was beaten up by the police,
with fists and rifle butts. The police had given a typically brutal,
awful demonstration of their prejudice. When, in fact, the police
realized that we were beginning to find out more than they wanted
exposed, they caught us by the elbows (and a policeman's grip can
be a very firm one indeed) and escorted us out. What fate awaited
Shakeel Ahmad I do not know, but I have little doubt that the
policemen took their revenge on him for having the temerity to
talk so frankly to us. Even assuming that Ahmad was guilty of
something and the policemen we talked to had nothing but vague
suspicion and reeking prejudice as their reasons for what they did,
what right did the policemen have to beat him up in such a fashion?

It was pure coincidence that our photographer was there, and we were there. But how many Shakeel Ahmads are there in Moradabad? Perhaps readers might begin to understand now why the minorities have so little faith in organizations like the PAC.

August 1980

Have Gun, Will Kill

In the autumn of 1981, Harijjans were killed in several villages in Uttar Pradesh. Two of these massacres — one in Dehuli, followed by another a few days later in Sarhupur —received widespread publicity. The killers who were Thakur Rajputs, had just one message to send through murder — the untouchable Jatav cobblers had to learn their place in society and the cast hierarchy.

★18 November 1981: Harijans massacred by Thakur gangs in a remote village in Mainpuri called Dehuli.

★24 November 1981: Utter Pradesh Chief Minister V. P. Singh promises to resign in a month's time if he cannot stop the dacoit (bandit) menace and end the insecurity of Harijans.

★13 December 1981: One of the Dehuli murderers, Santosha, arrested. The real culprit, Radhe, still free.

★24 December 1981: CM says things are much better; there is no need to resign.

★30 December 1981: Prime Minister Indira Gandhi agrees with UP CM; congratulates him.

★30 December 1981: In another remote village in Mainpuri, 37 km from Dehuli, a place called Sarhupur, unidentified armed men turn up, do not rob anyone, just shoot dead ten Harijan men, women and children.

Early in the morning, the winter mist sits heavily on the highway, now littered with the debris of a harsh night: crows and vultures picking greedily at the carcass of a dog which could not get out of the way of a flying truck; *dhabas* (roadside eating places) which have kept awake through the night now preparing to keep awake through the day; a shivering, heavily covered stranger waiting for a sympathetic truck to give him a left. This is the great Grand Trunk Road, now renamed the Sher Shah Suri Marg — a decision which must be recorded as the Charan Singh Government's sole contribution to art and culture. From Agra to Tundla to Ferozpur you travel east : so straight east that the rising orange sun, now gently dissolving the mist is right in front of your eyes, a glowing *bindiya* pasted on a light curving wall at the edge of vision. The early buses have begun picking up their handfuls of passengers at various stops. A little outside Ferozabad, four young men sprint quickly to reach a bus before it continues on its patterned journey. A perfectly normal sight, except for one thing. All the four men have guns slung across their backs. They are not dacoits; just ordinary people on some specific journey. What is abnormal is that that is not unusual everyone does not wear guns. The poor would like to, but just do not have them. Nor is it true that everyone who is well off always carries a weapon; there is no need for such cowboy western dramatics. But anyone who goes on a journey to unknown areas, or anyone with anything to protect, sees to it that a gun is within reach. That is the impact of the fear that has swept through the dacoit-infested districts of western Utter Pradesh : Agra, Etah, Mainpuri, Etawah, Kanpur. This is the land where the fate of many empires has been decided; a contiguous area which spreads over into the Bharatpur district of Rajasthan to the west, and into the famous Chambal to the south; this is the land of the Jamuna, extending into the Bhind and Morena districts of Madhya Pradesh. From the flourish and prosperity of Mathura and Agra (with its tubewells and tractors) the soil weakens, becoming increasingly saline in Mainpuri, sinking soft in Kanpur and burning rocky and dusty in the Chambal. The language spoken, by and large, is Brajbhasha or variations of it, with its distinct inflections separating it from Hindi-an extra 'o' at the end of a word, changing an initial 'w' to 'j' as for instance the 'wuh' of Hindi becoming the 'juh' of Braj. E.R.Neave, author of the Mainpuri (this is the district which contains the infamous Dehuli) volume of the District Gazetteer of the United Provinces, published by the British Government in 1910, remarks on 'the extraordinary homogeneity in language through the district, no less than 9,999 out of every 10,000 being returned as speaking western Hindi.' (The declared language of the 10,000th chap? Bengali.)

There are other elements of homogeneity in this area. The social dominance of the Rajput or Thakur caste, for instance; wars and militancy are in its blood; it is an armed caste and its members use their weapons to retain their place in the hierarchy. But the bulk of the population is made up of what are known as the backward castes: the Mallahs, whose villages dot the banks of the Jamuna as they live off the river (one such village, beautifully located where a small river flows into the vast Jamuna, is called Gorhapurwa, and from that village emerged a woman called Phoolan); the Ahirs; the Jats; the Gujjars; the Lodha Rajputs and so many others in a sequence of diminishing importance till you reach that shadow world of the outcaste, the untouchable. The people of the backward castes are hardworking, and excellent agriculturists; their women come out into the fields and work as hard as the men on the land. Their attitude is a classic example of the behaviour of the middle class. They resent the supremacy of the Thakur and the Brahmin, and are hostile to them, but what they do share with the upper castes is the same hatred for and contempt of the untouchable Harijan. If anything they are even more vicious against the Harijan.

It is only recently that the backwards have found some economic stability, with the rise in agricultural productivity and income. There has even been an attempt at the political consolidation of this section, represented by the emergence of the Lok Dal political party. This has, inevitably, only raised caste tensions; tensions have led to violence; money has been spent to buy guns; guns have been used to kill; killers have, sometimes, become outlaws (*farrar*) rather than spend a lifetime either in prison or as an easy target for the seekers of vengeance.

In this world where caste is such a dominant force, where violence is such a common occurrence, it is inevitable that the dacoit doubles as a protector of caste interests — in return for vital food and shelter.

This is as true of the past as it is of the present, particularly of the time when effective power lay in the hands of petty landlords. The dacoit gangs became the private armies of the castes, and sometimes these armies even became powerful enough to acquire pretensions, in which case they had either to be bribed into respectability, or be killed. Eric Hobsbawm, in his superb monograph, *Bandits* mentions two specific examples. In the 1830s, a dacoit called Gajraj ('risen from the profession of a monkeyshowman to be the Robin Hood of Gwalior') was given the ghats and the ferries of the Chambal so that he would not disturb the Durbar. The other near contemporary instance is of a Gujjar from Saharanpur, called Kallua, who became so rich and powerful that he eventually had about a 1,000 men under him. At which point he declared himself Raja Kalyan Singh (if the history of princes and princesses were not doctored by obsequious courtiers, how many would end up with similar origins?) and gave his actions a political and social colour: the warrior king of the Gujjars was challenging the White Man.

The White Man sent 200 Gurkhas; Raja Kalyan Singh, in a tragic display of nouveau riche valour, awaited the attack outside his fort, and was promptly slaughtered. The bandit-as-leader had gone too far. But he had left many children behind; those children have currently such names as Radhe and Santosha (Thakurs), Chabiram and Anar Singh (Ahirs or Yadavs), or Phoolan (Mallah). Radhe and Santosha got protection from the Thakurs when they were on the run; Phoolan was not found despite the year-long efforts of two State Governments because the Mallahs would not betray her (she surrendered later); Chabiram and Anar Singh could always find a safe bed in a Yadav village. (Because of this 'fraternal' feeling the UP State Government passed a rule that anyone giving food or shelter to dacoits would be considered guilty). Pandit Naiksa, the Brahmin dacoit, could always count on support and shelter from his religious brethren. A joke goes that the Brahmin caste is the only one which does not have its own gang of dacoits, since it actually controls all the gangs. How? Every dacoit gang has its chaplain; the Pandit (priest) is always around, and being a Pandit he will ensure that he has influenThe guru of the famous Man Singh was Pandit Ram Lal.

The most interesting thing to note, however, is no one can think of an important (or even unimportant) Harijan dacoit. The Harijan is too weak to even rob and kill on a respectable scale; his is a petty life which cannot be allowed to go beyond petty pleasures and petty sins. That is the true law of the land, on which everyone who is not a Harijan is agreed.

If this was a simple cops and robbers story, it could be told simply. But today's reality is a collage of many things. History has nurtured in the Thakur a superiority complex that makes him quite unable to disguise his contempt for the other castes, and the violent edge of that contempt is reserved particularly for the Jatavs (or the Chamars). The untouchable Jatav is touchable only when a pretty Jatav woman can be raped, or when a whimpering man has to be dragged to the field to do forced, whimsically paid labour. History has given the Thakur possession of weapons; once the sword, now the gun. But the dregs of recent agricultural prosperity have filtered down to the Jatavs, the most aggressive of the depressed and brutalized Harijan communities; the shoes they now cobble get a better price, there is the occasional beneficiary of the job reservation policy; a community which lived on the mercy of the upper castes, especially the landowning Thakurs, was suddenly able to find food from other sources. And this was, inevitably, enough to stir the first embers of rebellion against upper caste oppression. The older Jatavs just never had the confidence, even with a full stomach, to look the Thakur in the eye, but another generation was growing up. The Thakur has an extraordinary sense of pride: sometimes it is healthy, sometimes the manifestations stink of putrid arrogance. The Thakur's mythology (if not necessarily historical reality) places a high premium on the head being held high even if the price of a straight neck is a sword through it. In the district of Mainpuri, this tradition is particularly strong. The dominant Thakur clan of Mainpuri Chauhans claim they were created by the prayers of the great sage Vasistha to war against demons, and count among their ancestors the great Prithviraj Chauhan. The Bhadauria *taluqdars* (landlords) were an unending irritation to whoever ruled Delhi (no Thakur has ruled Delhi after Prithviraj Chauhan; incidentally, a state of affairs that Chandra Shekhar, the Thakur Janata MP, surely would like to rectify).

Among the problems of the head pointing skywards is that you can't see the land. It is an interesting fact that the Thakurs are very poor cultivators: their pride does not allow them to bend their head to do the kind of work necessary to make the land bountiful. The Lodhas (a backward caste) have no such hangups. The Gazetteer for Mainpuri notes: 'They (the Lodhas, a caste lower on the scale) are first rate cultivators and hold 7.45 per cent of the total cash rented area as tenants and a great deal more as subtenants of Thakurs and Brahmans, who cannot so far derogate from their dignity as to touch a plough.' On the other hand, the power of the Thakur made him the principal landowner. In 1910, the Thakurs formed 8.76 per cent of the population, but the percentage of area in their possession was 45.71 per cent. They still remain the most important landowners, though the percentages may have altered a little. The point is: Thakur landowners have traditionally needed labour for their farms, and the cheapest and most exploited labour was always the Harijan.

The Thakurs of Dehuli have, in fact, carved a niche for themselves in history; they were known for their independence, their ability and desire to fight. Let us turn again to Mr Neave's valuable account of this district: Dehuli, 'the chief seat of Barnahal, is mentioned in the *Tarikh-i-Mubarik Shah* as "the strongest place in the possession of the infidels" and as having been attacked and destroyed in 1420 A.D. by Sultan Khizr Khan on his march from Koil to Etawah. (They were) always noted for turbulence and recusancy...In the Mutiny, again, Ganga Singh of Dehuli, the recognized head of the family, rebelled, and his property was confiscated.'

It was this kind of Thakur, then, who was watching the growing impudence of the Jatavs. One of the unreported facts about the Dehuli massacre is that physical fights had broken out between the Thakurs and the Jatavs on the issue of forced labour. To the Thakur, this was as unimaginable as it was unacceptable: that world which had been so tightly bound for countless generations was coming to an end. And how would it end? Would it end with a bang or with a whimper? There was no way that the Thakur was going to allow it to end with a whimper; there would be a bang.

On 30 December 1981, Prime Minister Indira Gandhi went to Lucknow on an assignment she made a regular feature of her administration: a review of the performance of the State Government. But this was clearly not a work as usual affair. Mrs Gandhi was quite aware that her Chief Minister in UP had barely survived the public outcry after the shameful massacre of Harijans in Dehuli. She made it a point, therefore, at the press conference she addressed, to pat her loyal Chief Minister on the back and declare herself satisfied that he had done the job of protecting Harijans well enough to remain in office.

That bubble was being pricked at precisely the time it was being inflated. Just thirty-seven kilometres away from Dehuli in the same now famous, or infamous, district of Mainpuri, is a larger village called Sarhupur. Around the time that the Prime Minister was telling the world, through the press, that all was well in UP, particularly after the post-Dehuli anti-dacoity operations, three men entered the village, asked for specific directions and took a winding lane towards the segregated Harijan locality. They were armed with carbines and self-loading rifles; their aim was not to rob or loot but just to kill. To kill Harijans (we shall examine this incident in more detail in the next chapter) And they made doubly sure that there was no mistake about this because they specifically checked at each house whether it was a Harijan residence or not before their guns spat out hate and death. It was all over in fifteen minutes. By that time six women, four children and two men had become fresh victims of an oppression that had started innumerable centuries ago. Their cruel message delivered, the assailants calmly went back to the darkness from which they had emerged.

There was a delayed attempt by the ruling authorities to portray the Dehuli massacre as a sad, but explicable, example of intra-village rivalry, and not an instance of caste oppression. After all, the implication of admitting it to be a casteist massacre was that V.P.Singh, despite being a Thakur himself, had not even managed to control his own caste's lawlessness. It was being hinted that Radhe, a known dacoit, was just taking revenge on the Harijans of his village (Radhe, of course, was himself a resident of Dehuli) for having opposed him. But no such explanation was possible in Sarhupur. The village had never known any violent internal tension. The Harijans were supplicant, earning their frugal bread mainly by making bangles for the factories around nearby Ferozabad. The other castes of the village were as dazed as anyone else by this massacre, whereas there is sufficient evidence in Dehuli to hint that many of the other Thakurs had instigated Radhe to kill the Harijans 'to teach them a lesson.' The massacre at Sarhupur indicates that someone was still trying to teach the Harijans a lesson, and the lesson was that if they did not submit to the upper castes, if they tried to whip up public emotions, if they tried to use their leverage with Governments to end the oppression, their lives would not be safe anywhere, they would be swatted to death like flies in village after village, and for how long and how often could the police protect them in the dispersed, difficult-to-reach villages of the enormous area? What other rationale could there be for Sarhupur? Where personal enmity or simple theft is clearly not a factor, the only other reason has to be institutional enmity, whether the institution be class or caste.

True, what I have just written is a hypothesis, since the identity of the assassins is not specifically known. But let us now examine the hypotheses that were immediately churned out by the members of the UP Government — and it is a fact that they also did not know, when they made their analyses, who the assailants were. What is interesting is that the explanations immediately point to the extent caste has coloured the view in the State that claims to be the heart of this great country.

The police reached Sarhupur about three hours after the indiscriminate killings (the toll would have been much higher, but most of the Harijan men were participating in a meeting organized to demand a higher kerosene ration for heating the stoves they used to make bangles). By nightfall the administration had learnt the dimensions of the tragedy. An ebullient Chief Minister, still buoyant after the Prime Minister's praise, went into a depression after an afternoon visit to the village on 31 December, cancelled a scheduled press conference and rushed instead to meet the PM in Delhi. But his two Ministers for Home Affairs (both equally voluble), cabinet minister, Swaroop Kumari Bakshi, and Rajendra Tripathi, were not as shy about their opinions. Mr Tripathi promptly said that the killings were politically motivated.

What could this mean? In saying this, Mr Tripathi was quite directly charging the opposition parties with having used dacoits to kill Harijans in order to destroy the V.P. Singh Government. In other words he was saying that the political parties were instigating dacoits of the backward castes to kill Harijans. R.C. Takru, the Home Secretary, carried this a logical step forward. He told the press, once again without the remotest evidence, that the Anar Singh gang was suspected of having committed the carnage.

To anyone unfamiliar with Anar Singh, Mainpuri, west UP and Lucknow, that seems a harmless enough charge: after all, Anar Singh is a well-known dacoit of that region. But the sting is carefully hidden: Anar Singh is a Yadav dacoit, from the backward castes, not a Thakur. Mr Thakur was subtly delinking Dehuli from Sarhupur (before any evidence could establish the case either way). That tactic did not succeed: the State was soon buzzing with the rumour that the assailant might again be Radhe, winning his second battle against Harijans. After all, Radhe was still free, and no one was even claiming that the police had any idea of his whereabouts.

And this brings us to another vital truth about dacoits, anti-dacoity operations, the police and politicians. Dacoity really became big news, demanding state-level attention and creating national level excitement, with the appearance of a young and pretty woman called Phoolan. A victim of her beauty, one stormy night (the night really was stormy, even if that sounds a bit like a Hindi film), she was abducted by dacoits, and was forced to become the paramour of two Thakur gang leaders, Sri Ram and Lala Ram. She later fell in love with a dacoit from her own caste, Vikram Mallah; in revenge the Thakurs not merely brutally killed Vikram but publicly stripped her and humiliated her in a village called Behmai. Phoolan was obviously a woman of some character. She created her own gang, took help from other gangs antagonistic to The Thakurs, and in a highly dramatic and vindictive outrage, killed twenty Thakurs from Behmai. Everyone was stunned. Such a thing had never happened before: the ruling caste of Thakurs had always been inviolate. Free guns were given to the Thakurs of Behmai (nobody dares to give the Harijans guns when they get killed), and V.P. Singh and Arjun Singh, Chief Minister of Madhya Pradesh, conferred officially in the heart of the dacoit region and vowed to eradicate the menace from their States. Police were mobilized, and the great operation started.

These were the names of some of the important dacoit leaders of the region at the time we are speaking of : Malkhan Singh, Chabiram, Anar Singh, Pothi, Mahavira, Phoolan, Pandit Naiksa, Sri Ram, Lala Ram, Radhe, Santosha, Bhima, Nathi, Geetam Jat, Pan Singh Tomar. The only important victories for the police in the year-long anti-dacoity operation were the death of Pan Singh Tomar (credit to the MP police) and the arrest of Santosha.

However, the police gathered great statistics. By 24 December, the UP administration alone claimed that over 1,500 'notorious' dacoits had been killed in 'encounters' and more than 9,000 arrested. But who was killed and who was arrested? The important gangs still roamed, demanding their tributes, collecting their ransoms and a good number of those killed in 'encounters' were just innocents who, for one reason or the other, had fallen foul of the local, low-level police officers and constables. There is, in fact, an absolute feeling of terror in the villages, as no one knows who will become the next statistic. Sometimes the police do make a genuine error; more often, the victim of an encounter is really the victim of extortion or the victim of personal vengeance. The honest truth is that the major dacoits get protection not only from their caste brethren (this alone can never be totally sufficient against a motivated and honest police force), but also from another very powerful section of society —the politicians. Electoral politics has degenerated to a point where candidate after candidate has taken recourse to the easiest solution — take the help of the two armed sections of the community, the police and the dacoits.

It should be clarified right away that the ruling party is not alone guilty of using the support of dacoits in elections; leaders of the major opposition party of the region, the Lok Dal, have done exactly the same (though with less success, perhaps because they could not get the help of the police as well). But opposition parties are not called upon to solve problems; ruling parties are. And when members of the ruling party have already sold their souls to dacoits in return for a legislator's letterhead or a ministerial chair, it is difficult for them to be sufficiently enthusiastic about catching the dacoits — no matter how windy their rhetoric.

Vishwanath Pratap Singh, according to reputation and one's own limited knowledge, is a reasonably honourable man who really does want to end this horrible problem. But to really do that, he needs a firmer hand and more honest politics. He has tried so far to bribe the devil by supping with its nominees; he has to stop that. If he really wants to arrest Radhe and restore some sense of confidence among the terrified Harijans, he might try diverting his rigid attention from the wasteland of Mainpuri and search instead the list of legislators where he might discover the protectors of Radhe.

If you think that is too harsh, here is a story. This story was narrated to me, in all its detail, by a policeman who knew it by heart. His obvious request was that his name not be quoted.

In the city of Ferozabad (near both Dehuli and Sarhupur) lives a man the police consider a known criminal. He has not been fully convicted yet, but he has twenty-six cases pending against him, and he has been out on bail. Quite a few of the cases can't go very far because witnesses are afraid of the criminal's revenge, for the charges against him include murder. At the moment he has slipped arrest ; warrants have been issued but, as the policeman ruefully admitted, warrants are sometimes not executed for a variety of reasons, including political pressure. He is at the moment evading arrest for a case of murder committed on 16 November 1980. This known criminal was one of the main organizers of the welcome given by the ruling party to Rajendra Tripathi, the Minister of State for Home Affairs in Uttar Pradesh in October. He even shared the dais with the honourable minister, and used the occasion to abuse certain members of the administration. It is possible that Mr Tripathi may turn around and say that, in public life, it cannot be expected of a minister to know the full truth about everyone he meets. But Mr Tripathi was not born yesterday. In any case, how does one expect the police officials and the district administration to react when they see their own minister in the company of one of the most wanted men of the city?

Venality only breeds its genetically accurate children. When politicians, who are the bosses, openly consort with the outlaw, how can one hope that the police will be angelic? Corruption is now so endemic in the system that the ability of the State to mobilize its resources against the corruptors has virtually disappeared. Noble intentions arouse a snigger; promises couched in catch phrases (example the *Dasyu unmolan abhiyan* — Plan for Uplift) raise a yawn. If there is too much pressure from the political heavyweights for 'results' so that some bleeding heart might be bandaged, then 'results' will be manufactured to order. Statistics are required, not qualitative analysis, and there can never be a shortage of statistics in a poverty-ridden, inaccessible land where a sense of a accountability has rarely existed. In any case villages like Dehuli or Sarhupur live outside the law of the Indian Penal Code, for who can endorse that order? Phoolan kills 20 Thakurs; how many Mallahs or backwards must be killed in order to assuage the heart of the Thakur? Don't worry, they'll be killed.

And, if sometimes the guardians of law and order themselves find dacoity a more lucrative source of income than bribes? Where all sense of morality has melted in the witches' cauldron, where honesty has become a fool's virtue, who will call whom a villain?

*

West of Agra, on the border of Rajasthan, is a Mallah hamlet called Purasurajmal. In the twilight of one morning in November the police came. Searching for a man called Rustam. Early in November, Rustam, not a very savoury character apparently, had gone drinking with a person called Padma, a young Thakur from a village in Rajasthan; after that session in a rural *theka* (country liquor shop), Padma disappeared. The police could not find Rustam; perhaps the Mallahs would not give him up. So the police vented their anger by looting about half a dozen houses of the better off Mallahs. Chet Ram, whom we spoke to, was one of the victims. He went to a fellow Mallah who had become a leader of Agra district, who made some sympathetic noises. That was all. But who will be heard when the din of other problems — the wails of widowed Harijan women, the anguished screams of dacoit victims, the silent terror of oppressed castes rocks the foundations of life? Chet Ram had to accept what had happened.

One of the interesting asides to this story is that the police and the dacoits wear the same uniform. The police, of course, wear their official uniform because that is the Government order. The dacoits have similar uniforms stitched for themselves as a disguise, so that when they approach a village to commit a dacoity the villagers may not be able to distinguish them from the police until it is too late. A feeling is growing that this visual ambiguity is now becoming the true reality, that there is not much difference between the dacoit and the policeman when it comes down to their behavior with the people. It will be a dangerous day when this suspicion becomes a conviction. Does Vishwanath Pratap Singh have a hand firm enough to prevent this much larger danger? Or is he willing to allow the police any liberty in return for statistics?

*

There is plenty of humbug in hell.' That was Shaw, in *Man and Superman*. Uttar Pradesh may not be quite as bad as the address Shaw was referring to, but by Satan, there is no shortage of humbug. The Harijan in Uttar Pradesh is asking for his life, and Vishwanath Pratap Singh is offering him electricity. The Harijan is screaming that all the upper castes hate him, rape him, and will never allow him to possess the one thing he wants even more desperately perhaps than food — self respect. And Mr Singh (in this respect, like any other politician, whether Charan Singh or Vajpayee) shows the Harijan a calculator which can work out all the caste and subcaste alliances that make up a victory in an election. The demand is for inspired social change, and the answer is a few more crumbs in the hope that this simpleton will be satisfied.

The twenty-four martyrs of Dehuli generated a whole bonanza of crumbs for that particular village. Dehuli is adjacent to a canal, which is why some kind of a track always existed for the bullock cart or later the cycle to follow the canal and reach the main road. You have to leave the metalled road that stretches from Ferozabad to Pratappur and turn right onto this track. The soil is so soft that an Ambassador's wheels churn up huge clouds of it; the wheel sinks treacherously into the mud, and the driver dare not keep the direction of the car straight but has to slowly zigzag his way to help the car retain some grip on the road. There are bumps and turns, and the car could easily get stuck on an unexpected, hard, foot-high ridge, leaving the front and back wheels spinning while you are stuck helplessly. And when you get stuck here you are helpless.

But now there are sudden signs of activity on this track — they are making it a road.

You walk down from this raised track for a few hundred yards to a village which, like every other village in the world, looks totally at peace with itself and its environment. Just outside the village is the Shiva temple: this is where the gangs of Radha and Santosha camped and feasted and drank before beginning their orgy of blood. The temple is quite intact, although before we reached Dehuli, we too had heard the story being spread across the State that the Harijans, in revenge against the massacre, had destroyed the sacred temple. (Another bit of insidious propaganda: that they burnt a Quran in one of the Muslim houses of the village; this too is a lie.) At the entrance to Dehuli is a raised platform on which are placed consecrated stones; these represent the deities the villagers especially invoke for the protection of the village.

Dehuli still largely empty. Not many of the Thakurs who left the village on 17 November, when the Santosha gang arrived, have returned yet, though a few of them have come back. That evokes the first important question: why had they left on the 17th when the massacre took place only on the 18th? Was it because they knew what was coming? But if there are not enough insiders, there are enough outsiders. There is a strong police contingent. And there are labourers busy building the community houses (government financed). But more impressive are the electricians setting up lines on sophisticated prefabricated cement poles: Dehuli is going to have electricity: Roads, electricity, water: what more could anyone in Dehuli want?

There is a macabre joke going around the villages these days: if you want development, either become a part of the Chief Minister's electoral constituency or kill a few Harijans. The Harijans themselves, with the practical native intelligence of the villager, point out the Catch-22 of all this 'development.' Prabhu Dayal, who has a job in Agra, told us in Dehuli that because they (Harijans) had died the village was getting benefits, but who would the benefits benefit most? Who would make the most of the electricity? Obviously the man with land and money to purchase a tubewell. Whose children would utilize the better school facilities most? Obviously the Thakur's. And in Sarhupur the villagers openly and violently displayed their disgust at the hypocrisy of the VIPs and ministers (scores of them have predictably been trooping out there to show their 'sympathy' and bribe the bereaved back into the ruling party fold). When Brij Nath Kuril, the Revenue Minister for UP (and also a Harijan), turned up at Sarhupur the angry Harijans surrounded him, made a public bonfire of all the gifts he had brought (blankets, woollen jerseys, etc) and refused to let him leave the village. They wanted assurances of protection, not cheap gimmicks.

The humiliated minister finally escaped in a police jeep!

Prabhu Dayal in Dehuli was openly sceptical of the ability or the willingness of the ruling party to punish Radhe and Santosha. How could they, he asked, when he had himself seen Santosha campaigning for the Congress (I) candidate in the 1980 State elections? Dayal was convinced that Santosha had merely been protected by this farce of an arrest, and that Radhe, protected by his caste and big political mentors, would go unpunished too — some way or the other would be found to get both off the hook.

Of course, the gestures have been made. We visited Radhe's house in Dehuli. The police, in a silly display of bravado, had smashed the locked door, and ransacked the belongings in search of "clues". The problem was elsewhere, and socio-political and real answers were elsewhere too. But since the Government is not interested in mentioning (at least publicly) the vital questions, one can hardly expect its functionaries to spend their ability and energy towards searching for real solutions.

The problem is the Harijan's search for bread with dignity. The problem is the complete unwillingness of the whole range of upper castes, and particularly the Thakurs who are in dire need of Harijan labour for their lands to give the Harijan the right to ask questions, the right to defend his women, the right to control his time: after all the day this society gives the Harijan honour, the Harijan will defend that honour. The Harijan is already asking for arms to protect his life: no Government, and certainly not the Thakur Government of V.P. Singh, dare give him guns. But there is a difference now. A post-independence generation has emerged among the Harijans which just might decide to retaliate with knives if necessary rather than be smashed like the mouse which had dared to question the supreme authority of man.

The caste problem of this region is not restricted to just the anti-Harijan feeling (though one must repeat, at the cost of sounding boring, that the one thing that does unite all the other castes is their contempt for the untouchable). The politics and rewards of casteism are taking their toll in virtually every sphere. One of the most serious fights at the upper echelons of life is the fight for power between the Thakurs and the Brahmins. This is not simply a fight for the Chief Ministership, but a fight for authority down the line. That is, if a Brahmin is in real charge, then the Brahmins down the line (in the districts, in the police force, etc) reap the benefits.

Then there is the powerful confrontation between the upper castes and backwards, who are a newly dominant force in the region. One of the signs of their power is of course the Lok Dal; the other important sign is that most of the gangs that roam these districts of west Uttar Pradesh (as distinct from Madhya Pradesh where Thakur gangs are still dominant) are from the backward castes: Chabiram, Anar Singh et al. The Thakurs have ,in fact, tried to promote Radhe,Santosha, Lala Ram and Sri Ram in a effort to counter the power which the backward caste dacoits were giving to their castes.

Change always demands a heavy price from society. It would be an exaggeration to say that what we are witnessing today in Uttar Pradesh is the first sign of any major revolution; it would be more accurate to describe it as yet another brutal attempt to stop that first sign of change from ever appearing on the horizon. The upper castes have the past and the present; they want to ensure that the future also remains with them. They have already usurped the glory of history and the wealth of the land; they do not want to surrender either. Like all social wars, the lines are often hazy; events seem to defy logic; and always, always the administrations try to misinterpret reality so that another palatable excuse might be possible, some more time might be purchased from the future. The upper castes have the guns. In the grab-what-you-can spirit of the present they will often use the guns against one another; they will barter, they will make peace; they will display the normal greed that determines so much human action; they will use the necessary cunning to ˚sue for settlement when the occasion demands.

But against one enemy, those who have guns will use them only to kill. That enemy is the wretched of the earth, the untouchable Harijan. And the Harijan must die without a cry of pain; the woman with a two-month-old child in Sarhupur must submit without anguish; the child must bleed without tears; the widow of Dehuli must willingly accept that this is her destiny and death will be the fate of those who want to change it; and the man must keep his head permanently bowed till natural or sudden death rids him of a life he never lived.

January 1982

A Tale of Two Villages

On the night of 31 December 1981, a gang of three upper caste Hindus armed with automatic weapons went on the rampage in a Chamar (cobbler) Harijan locality on the outskirts of Sarhupur, an isolated village in Uttar Pradesh. At the same time Satyajit Ray released his classic film based on Premchand's Sadgati.

The first tale was written by that master, Premchand*, and it is about Dukhi Chamar and his young wife Jhuria. The second story is about a woman who has just stepped into her twenties, a woman called Narayani. The first story is set in the 1920s. The second belongs to an India which has a Constitution with a lot of words written in it. In the last week of December 1981, Satyajit Ray began showing, to select audiences, a short film he had made from a Premchand story, *Sadgati* (Deliverance): in this the master of cinema had powerfully etched out the pain and silence and death rattle of Dukhi Chamar. Coincidentally, towards the end of that same week of December, on the 30th, in the still-unknown village of Sarhupur, in the gathering chill of dusk, the tragedy of Narayani was enacted. Both the villages belong to that world which Mahatma Gandhi described to his dear countrymen as the 'real India'; in both the stories, the objects of torture and death were the people the Mahatma had christened 'The Children of God': Harijan. Premchand, Satyajit Ray, Sarhupur: art and life were a mirror to each other; time and pious resolutions had changed nothing; the real India still lived out its awful realities.

Art: Sadgati — *Opening Sequence*

The calm and still soft light of a summer morning; the worry on

---

*Premchand was the pseudonym of the great Hindi novelist, Dhanpat Rai.

Jhuria's face is at odds with the freshness and serenity of the environment. She turns to her twelve-year-old daughter, Dhania, an exquisitely beautiful child, just a moment or two away from adulthood, and asks her where her father is. Dhania is sweeping the courtyard; she pauses to answer that her father has gone to cut some grass. Irritation furrows Jhuria's forehead. Muttering, she struts off to look for Dukhi Chamar: there he is, doing the only thing he knows, cutting grass, his face and body already tired by work, a debilitating fever, and the lack of food. Doesn't he know that he has to go to Pandit Ghasiram's house to invite the priest over so that an auspicious date can be fixed for Dhama's marriage? Dukhi looks hard at his wife, a touch of anger inflaming his nostrils: what did she think he was cutting the grass for? After all, he could not go to the great Pandit's house empty-handed, could he? In any case, why didn't she go about finishing her own work? Where would the Pandit sit when he came? He would never sit on an untouchable's cot. So what arrangements had she made to solve that problem?

Jhuria: even an untouchable's existence has not robbed her of innocence; she wants to borrow a cot from the headman! Dukhi tells her the facts of her life: she wouldn't get a coal to light a fire with from them, not to speak of a cot. Dukhi picks up the bundle of grass, stumbles a little under the load; Jhuria runs to help him. Dukhi then tells her all she must do while he goes to fetch the Pandit. He will bring some *mahua* leaves, which are considered holy, and she must make a leaf mat on which the Pandit can sit, and a leaf plate on which they can keep some food as a gift to the priest. Jhuria must take the daughter of the Gond (who is touchable) to the village Sahu's shop and ask her to buy for them all the things they need: a seer of *atta*, half a seer of rice, one *pao* of dal, half a *pao* of ghee, salt, haldi(turmeric), and then she must remember to keep four annas in one corner of the plate.

And she must remember to never, never touch anything! *Nahin to gajab ho jaayega*!

Dukhi refuses to eat anything in case it gets late–it's a good mile to the Brahmin's house, and he might miss Panditji if he delays. Anyway, it's only a question of bringing him to the house. He will not take very long, Dukhi says, and she must get everything done before he gets back.

Reality: Sarhupur — 30 December 1981

The winter winds chill the bone in the flat land that sweeps away south from the Himalayas, adding a corrosive edge to the temperature which is hovering single digit degrees above zero. By six-thirty, the sun, a late departer in the north, has finally gone down, taking away its warmth; the world is slipping through the gauze of dusk into the darkness of a night decorated with an unfathomable profusion of stars, bright but not warm. Now the fires are being lit for the men to huddle around and exchange the day's gossip. The women are in the kitchen preparing whatever food their means allow them.

Narayani's three-year-old son, a confident, vocal, lovable brat, has had, like the rest of his family, only fried potatoes for the afternoon meal. The only food available is potatoes, and Narayani is preparing to cook them for dinner too. Three-year-old Daya-shankar begins protesting;he wants some *roti* along with the *aloo* (potatoes). Narayani's heart cannot say no, and she asks her husband Raghuvar Dayal to go to the village (as everywhere else in the country, the Harijans are not allowed to live in the main village, but granted a humiliating space on the outskirts) to borrow a cupful of *atta* (flour) so that she can make the *roti*. Raghuvar Dayal leaves to get the flour.

There are not many men in the Harijan *basti* at that moment. Almost all of them are at a meeting taking place at Mangalsingh Jatav's place. It is an important meeting: they want to make a joint appeal to the Government for a higher kerosene ration for the stoves they use to shape the bangles which give them their livelihood. The Harijans do not have land; they work either as landless labourers, or for the flourishing and famous bangle industry of nearby Ferozabad. This meeting will save their lives.

Now the shadows have become dark enough to camouflage a stranger's face; from the haze settling over the field emerge three young men. They wear police uniforms; their faces are partially masked; one has a torch; all have guns — sophisticated weapons, including the SLR and .30 carbine. They find an old woman trudging back to the village; they ask her the way to the Harijan *basti* (settlement). She points vaguely in the direction, and runs away, terrified. Santoshi, a child still not in her teens, is returning from the fields when these three young men catch her: '*Ai morhi, Chamaran ka mohalla kaun sa hai?*'(Kid, where is the place where the Chamars live?) She replies that the *Jatavs* live there. A hard slap across her face. '*Jatav nahin*, Chamar', they say. They are punishing her for using the more respectable term for these Harijans, she has called them *Jatavs*, and not Chamars.

Then they turn into a narrow lane which will take them to the *basti* of the Harijans, and to an appointment with murder.

Art: Sadgati — *A Priest's Price.*

The sandalwood lines must be drawn with love and confidence and care; after all, this is the paint which is the source of the Brahmin's power, not to mention his ballooning belly. Pandit Ghasiram is a master of this art, and is in no hurry to finish his decorations. He then goes through his morning *puja*, while his wife, the plump Lakshmi (Panditji's third wife; the other two have died — it was the will of the gods), sits on the inner verandah peeling vegetables for the afternoon meal. A barking dog announces the arrival of the morning's first visitor. His *puja* over, Pandit Ghasiram pours himself a glass of comforting *bhang* to help him through the day, then goes out to enquire why the dog is barking. He finds Dukhi Chamar waiting there, sitting on his haunches.

Dukhi immediately prostrates himself before the *maharaj*. The priest, bored, concentrates on his *bhang*. Ah, so that Chamar wants him to find an auspicious date. Ghasiram's son, school-books in hand, comes out and stops to watch what is happening. Pandit Ghasiram howls: 'What are you stopping for? Get going or you'll be late for school again!' There is no need for a child to see an untouchable Chamar unless he is absolutely forced to.

'You think I am free to go anytime anybody wants me to go anywhere?' Pandit Ghasiram asks Dukhi, stalling for time: his mind is elsewhere, searching for profit and loss. 'You will have to wait,' the priest tells the Chamar, and there is a glint of relief in the Chamar's eyes: the holy priest has said yes, he has said he will come, all he wants me to do is wait a little!

'Well,' says the priest, 'since Dukhi will have to wait a bit why doesn't he use his time to sweep the front of the house?' 'Of course, *maharaj*, of course.' And where should he keep the bundle of grass he has brought as an offering?' In front of the cow, you dimwit, where else?'

Sweeping comes easily to the Chamar, after all the human race has kept him alive only to clean its dirt. Dukhi finishes his work quickly and calls out, 'Maharaj! Dukhi has completed his sweeping.'

'Oh. In that case, there is a pile of hay which has to be carried across the field to the fodder bin. It's a bit of a distance but what's that for a tough chap like Dukhi? And listen : after the hay is done, split some wood, will you? There's a log outside, under the tamarind tree, which has to be chopped up into small bits.'

Dukhi stares at the hay, and the first signs of despair now begin to appear on his emaciated face. Dukhi has never learnt to know anger; but he has known despair many times, so many times.

In the meantime, pretty, chirpy, playful Dhania, quite excited by the importance of the day but desperately trying not to show it, desperately trying to remain the child who plays hopscotch, has made a lovely plate out of the *mahua* leaves. And Pandit Ghasiram is giving a lesson from the Gita to a young chap whose wife has died (text for the day: so what?). Dukhi, very tired and very helpless, comes again to the door to be met with an irritable, 'Have you chopped the wood?' No.' Dukhi does not know where the axe is. He is told; he finds the axe. It is not a very heavy axe, and the blade is blunt, but Dukhi picks it up and goes to search for the huge log of wood which he must chop into small bits in order that a priest may come to his doorstep and the command of a religion that has placed him on the level of excrement might be obeyed.

Reality: Sarhupur — *Flies in the Night.*

The killers come quickly through the lane to the space where the Harijan houses begin, and stop. About half-a-dozen yards away, from inside her hut, 50-year-old Chameli's daughter-in-law has told her, 'Mother, put the buffalo in; it will become dark.' Chameli has just stepped out of her hut when one of the killers comes in her way. A question mark appears on the old woman's face. The answer comes immediately: two bullets, one in her neck and one in her chest. The old woman drops dead. Her daughter-in-law shrinks back into the darkness of the hut and hides under the khatiya (cot).

Krishan Swaroop is lying on a *dalaan*; hearing the staccato burst of bullets he drops down and hides in the tub meant for the buffalo's food, and witnesses the theatre of assault and death.

To the right of Chameli's hut is Ram Swaroop's, and his son Prem Singh, in his late twenties, is standing outside the door. Scared, nonplussed, trembling, he asks the killers, 'Thakur Sahab, have we done anything?" The answer is a rattle of bullets: Prem Singh falls. Prem Singh's mother, Baikunthi, cannot believe her eyes: all she understands is that her son has just been alive, and for some inexplicable reason someone has come from somewhere and now blood is spurting out of his body. She cries out, 'Lalla (an affectionate way of calling out to a loved child), stay still: I'll wipe all that blood,' and leaps towards her son. Baikunthi is the next one to die.

Now the killers turn to search for fresh quarry; they separate — two remain together, and one goes another way. The single killer walks towards the house of Ram Bharose, his wife Premvati, twelve-year-old Sukhdevi, ten-year-old Harishankar, and seven-year-old Kailash. Young Sukhdevi is cooking a *roti* on a *tawa*, and her brothers are around her, waiting for the food to get ready. They are all stunned into silence by the gunfire. The gun opens up ratatatatatat. In a flash the three children are dead: the left side of Harishankar's face is blown off and thrown against the wall (many days later the blood still makes macabre patterns on the light brown mud walls, and the bread that 12-year-old Sukhdevi was cooking for her brothers has gone black but is still lying there, mute testimony to a strange whirlwind). The mother, Premvati, is still breathing, but virtually dead; Ram Bharose is given up for dead by the killer but miraculously survives with only minor wounds. The killer moves on.

The other two have gone to the hut of Ram Prasad, the next arbitrary spot where Harijans are available for massacre. The single killer, now finished with the murder of three children, stands outside Raghu Dayal's house, next to Ram Prasad's. Parvati is cooking food inside her hut; she has heard the gunfire but is too slow to react (unlike many of the children who had run for shelter the moment they realized what was happening), as are her eighteen-year-old son, Suresh, and her twenty four-year-old daughter-in-law Sheela. The adults pay the price for adult curiosity and concern. In a moment they are dead. The killers see another Harijan woman, Saguna Devi. She too is killed. It is exactly fourteen minutes since they have entered the *mohalla* to kill whichever Harijan they could find.

Who were the killers? No one knew. Why had they come to kill these Harijans? No one knew. Had the Harijans done anything, anything to suffer such a fate? Nothing. Had they even raised their eyes against anyone from the upper caste? No. Then why had young men, old women, young women, alive and smiling children, been snuffed out like flies whimsically smacked to death? Their only crime was that they had been born Harijans. And someone was once again sending out a message, a message that was as old as history could recall. The message was that Harijans would live and die, work or perish, at the behest of their superiors; they had no existence of their own, except as completely dehumanized slaves.

It took fifteen minutes for the three young killers who had come from the darkness to sound out their message in that special Morse code of the gun. After these fifteen minutes they turned their attention to a woman called Narayani.

Art: Sadgati — *Death in the Afternoon*

The grass had bowed easily to Dukhi's scythe but this obstinate, huge chunk of wood is another matter. This massive trunk has supported the birth and rebirth of fruit and leaves for generations; even fallen, it is formidable. Dukhi's fully-swung axe simply glances off the body, without even puncturing the skin of the wood. And now his hunger and feverishness are demanding their price too. It is past noon; Panditji is in the cool of his verandah eating his lunch while his wife gently fans him; Dukhi wants to go home too and eat, but home is more than a mile away, and Panditji might get very angry if he stops chopping the wood and maybe he will not come home to find an auspicious date for Dhania's wedding. He must chop this wood,he must. Damn. That grass surrenders easily enough. Why doesn't this wood give way? He is perspiring freely now, and gasping, and he sits down to rest; then he gets up, and now he can't raise his hands,and his feet are trembling, a shadow falls under his eyes, and butterflies are fluttering in his head. But

Dukhi keeps on at his job. He wants something: perhaps a smoke would restore him, give him some more strength. A passing Gond is staring at him: why doesn't that damn Brahmin give you something to eat? the Gond asks. How could Dukhi dare to ask for food? Then whack away, says the Gond disgustedly. Some tobacco and a pipe: could the Gond give him that? Yes.

Dhania and Jhuria are waiting. Sleep creeps into Jhuria's eyes as she slumps against a wall in front of her house. Dhania is quite happy playing hopscotch.

Dukhi, his *chilam* and tobacco in hand, calls out to the Pandit, still eating his expansive meal. Dukhi has accidentally wandered to the threshold of the Pandit's house and is actually sitting on his haunches a step inside. 'What you want now?' Could I have a coal?' asks Dukhi.

Pandit Ghasiram controls his irritation and tells his wife Lakshmi to give him a light. But the Panditayin is not able to control herself, and she screams in anger at her husband, loud enough for the Chamar to hear: ' You have got so lost in your charts that you have lost all sight of your religion. Chamar, dhobi, Pasi anyone, it seems, can lift his head and enter our house these days. This isn't a Hindu's home anymore; it has become a resthouse. Tell that scoundrel to get out or I will scorch his face with a firebrand. He wants fire, doesn't he !,

Pandit Ghasiram counsels patience. 'He has just stepped in; well, so what has happened? The earth is holy and beyond uncleanliness. He hasn't touched anything of yours. Give him a little fire; after all he is doing our work.' And then Pandit Ghasiram produces his clinching argument. 'If you had got someone else to chop that wood, you would have had to pay four annas at least.' The argument is settled, and the Pandit's wife, face averted from the unpleasant sight of a Chamar at such a close distance, brings the coal on a clutch, but she can't resist the temptation of throwing the burning coal at Dukhi. It lands on his head and singes him.

But Dukhi isn't upset by that. Instead, he is upset with himself. It was wrong of him, he thinks, to enter the house. How can a Chamar enter a Pandit's house? After all, these people are so holy and clean, that is why the world gives them so much prestige, so much power. They are not Chamars. He had grown so old in this very village, and yet he had not even learnt so much! Which is why when the Panditayin throws the coal, Dukhi treats it as if it was a gift from heaven itself. He prostrates himself at her feet, and cries out, 'Mother, it was a great mistake on my part that I entered your house. I have, after all, only a Chamar's sense. If we Chamars were not such fools, why would we get kicked around so much?'

The Chamar's tears touch some vague chord in Lakshmi. She goes back to her place beside her husband, who is still chewing his cud, and after he has finally finished, tells her husband to give the Chamar something to eat. 'Are there any *rotis* left,' asks the Pandit. 'A couple.' 'Oh, just that. What use are a couple of *rotis* to a Chamar? These fellows, when they eat, need at least a seer of flour.'

'One seer! Forget it,' says Lakshmi, 'who is going to go to such a bother in this heat for a Chamar?'

Dukhi drags heavily at the *chilam*, trying desperately to draw nourishment out of smoke. Soon the smoke is over too, and Dukhi goes back to chopping the virulent wood. Pandit Ghasiram rinses his mouth thoroughly of the stains and particles of the meal, and then lays himself down to the comfort of sleep and snores. And for half an hour without pause, his anger rising in direct proportion to his ineffectiveness, Dukhi hammers away at the unanswering tree trunk. Suddenly Dukhi loses his temper, and flings the axe away. The axe arcs towards the mud path on which an aghast Brahmin, passing by, ducks to avoid it. Dukhi is amazed at himself: how did he get angry? What has he done! He runs to retrieve the axe, and apologizes profusely to the Brahmin. The Brahmin is too stunned to say anything. Another rushes up to him to ask what has happened. 'He threw-an-axe-at-me!.. He must have gone berserk.'

(Let us now pause in our narrative, and assume that Dukhi belongs to the Age of the Crocodile Tear and Shameless Cover up. The story of his death is picked up by a journalist, and quickly gets national publicity. The Chief Minister of Uttar Pradesh, accompanied by his Home Minister and the Inspector General of Police, gets into the State helicopter and lands at the quickly constructed helipad. He goes straight to Jhuria's house and announces a grant of Rs. 10,000 for Jhuria, a peon's job for Dhania's husband-to-be, and roads and electricity for the village. Now the milling journalists ask why Dukhi died. The Chief Minister pulls a long face, says that what happened is very sad, but we must see things in perspective: the Brahmins of the village are not totally to blame for the tragedy. Why? Well, you see, it seems that Dukhi, apart from being a very ill man — he had very bad fever — should not have offered of his own accord (mark that phrase: that is a favourite phrase of the establishment when it wants to cover up) to work for Pandit Ghasiram who, after all, was willing to pay him handsomely in addition to generously helping him out by fixing an auspicious date for Dhania's wedding. Plus, now this is slightly embarrassing, but we have to say it in the interests of truth, Dukhi was also mad. The fever had clearly affected his brain. There are witnesses who saw him throw an axe at a Brahmin who was passing by while he was working. According to some people, it was Dukhi who was trying to start a caste war actually... The next day newspaper headlines dutifully parrot that. The Home Minister comes down from Delhi and announces that it was all really an old family feud, but Harijans should be armed. His Minister of State promptly denies that there is any plan to arm Harijans. The Prime Minister then blames the Opposition for starting vicious rumours. But now back to Premchand's short story and Satyajit Ray's film.)

Dukhi becomes overcome with weariness, and his eyes close on brimming tears; he breaks down and sobs.

Pandit Ghasiram's eyes open. He blinks twice to adjust himself to the sunlight, gets up, gargles, washes his face, tucks a paan into one side of his mouth and comes out of the house. And what does Pandit Ghasiram see when he comes out? That Chamar,Dukhi, sleeping! And that block of wood is still unchopped, in fact it is exactly as it was. Pandit Ghasiram gets angry. So this is what Dukhi did the moment his back was turned! The saying was perfectly true: let the *neech* (low) get a full stomach and they would begin looking the other way. He orders Dukhi to get back to work.

Now a passion surges through Dukhi, a rage which inflames the heart and rushes to the head. He must defeat that block of wood. Hit it. Harder. And Pandit Ghasiram, his hands on his hips, begins keeping time to the frenzied strokes of the axe: yes, harder, that's it, harder, there, it will crack now. Content that Dukhi is finally doing enough, Pandit Ghasiram goes in for his afternoon ablutions and bath. Dukhi has lost his senses. He begins *atta*cking the wood wildly, as if all the tiredness, the hunger, the fever, had never been. Half-an-hour, and the wood finally cracks. Dukhi's head begins spinning. The axe slips out of his grasp.

Dukhi falls down. Dead.

Reality: Sarhupur — *The Rape of Narayani.*

Three-year-old Dayashankar is a chirpy child; he does not need encouraging to talk to us. '*Main to darey bhaag gaya tha. Goli maar dete,*' he tells us; there are not many three-year-olds in the country with any concept of bullets or death or escape, but life has already told Dayashankar some basic truths about his existence. It is Dayashankar who wanted *roti* from his mother, Narayani, and it is because she sent off her husband Raghuvar Dayal to borrow some flour that Dayal was saved. But to return to the events of that fateful day. Dayashankar runs away to hide before the killers can reach Narayani's house; but she can't escape fast enough since she has a two-month-old baby with her. The three killers enter her house. Narayani is not particularly pretty, as urban concepts of beauty go, but she is young and attractive. The nature of the hunger switches from murder to rape. Narayani tries to run, but one killer catches her and says, 'You come with us,' and starts dragging her. She cries, 'Why are you beating us poor people?' The reply is two hard slaps and another question: 'Where is your man?' She tells them that he has gone to get some food. 'Then what are you doing here? Come with us.'

Narayani pleads that she has a two-month child she cannot leave behind. But who is listening? (Narayani tells us later that, instinctively, she told the killers that her two-month-old baby was a daughter; in reality it is a boy but she was afraid that if she mentioned it was a boy they would kill the baby; a girl they would ignore, which is exactly what they did.) They drag her out and take her into the fields.

As they are leaving, one of the killers mutters, 'Where have all the bastards disappeared? There should have been fifty to sixty here. It seems we will have to come again.' They keep Narayani with them for half-an-hour, and let her go. They then disappear into the darkness from which they had come.

The drama had lasted a little less than an hour. The rattle of gunfire had repeatedly destroyed the silence of the countryside, and was clearly heard as far away as Makhanpur (about five kilometres from Sarhupur). Sarhupur itself was a fairly large village, and a reasonably well-off one. There were at least five families with licensed guns. The most respected village elder, a Pandit, later described to us how he first learnt that there was some trouble in the Harijan *basti*: 'First, I thought that someone was beating a loud drum. Then I realized that this was gunfire. Later I realized that so many had been killed. All the villagers then forced me to go there to show some sympathy. Frankly, in all these years I have never been to that area; I didn't know what it looked like; this was the first time in my life that I was going to a Chamar *basti*.'

No one wanted to, or perhaps could, come to the help of the Harijans who had become the latest statistics in an age old manhunt.

Art: Sadgati — *A Post Mortem.*

Moti, on his way back from school, has stopped to watch this mad Chamar at work, and watched him die. He peers, senses something is wrong, and goes inside to tell his father, 'The Chamar is dead.' Pandit Ghasiram doesn't believe it; he goes out and in a moment can see that his son is right. The Gond is watching it all. Pandit Ghasiram realizes what he has done; his face becomes as white as his *dhoti*; he panics.

Inside, Lady Lakshmi Macbeth is far more calm. 'Well,' she says, 'there is only one thing to do. Send word to the Chamars to come and take the corpse away (nobody else will touch the untouchable corpse).' Ghasiram is still mumbling guiltily. hat are you mumbling for? He was chopping wood and died. He must have been ill. It doesn't mean you are responsible. Some people die in their sleep. You didn't know he would die.' The rationalization is perfect, and the intellectual Brahmin is, of course, now quite convinced that it is all right.

But a crisis far greater than the death of a mere Chamar is brewing. Dukhi has died just outside Pandit Ghasiram's house, and that is where his body is lying. So no Brahmin can use that road until that untouchable and unseeable body is removed. Even that would not be so much of a problem, except that the body is lying smack in the way to the well. So until that body is removed, no one can go to get any water.

Pandit Ghasiram, a little queasy, even shaken, gathers himself and takes a stance: about twenty yards away are the Chamar men, standing immobile, sullen, mute, defiant. Pandit Ghasiram breaks the silence with effort: 'Dukhi died a little while ago outside my house. If you could arrange to have his body removed...I was about to go to his house with him when he died quite suddenly. The body can't lie there indefinitely. So please arrange to have it removed.'

No one answers, no one budges. The Gond has come and told them all. He has told them about the Pandit's inhumanity, and he has also warned them that this might become a police case, and no one should touch the body-or there will be a frame-up.

The Chamars can understand that. No one moves. Pandit Ghasiram goes back. Lakshmi is waiting for him, anxiously. He reports his failure. 'Nonsense,' says Lakshmi, 'they don't expect us to remove it, do they?' Good question. 'So what happens now?', Lakshmi asks. 'I don't know,' replies Pandit Ghasiram simply.

Dhania's world has stopped; Jhuria's world has shattered. There are some tragedies in which words have no meaning. One can either stand totally benumbed, looking at nothing, saying nothing, hearing nothing, because now nothing exists; or one can let the wound bleed in an unending primal wail that finally exhausts the body even if it does nothing to lighten the heart. Dhania is silent; Jhuria wails. A storm has replaced the sun; rain has turned the soft mud into putty. She races towards her dead husband and clings to his lifeless body; Jhuria implores the dead man: 'Open your eyes. Oh, why don't you open your eyes! What a curse this is and our only daughter just about to be married! Why did you have to be so cruel! Leaving us when we needed you most!' Then, in a gesture of impotent fury, she hurls herself against the closed door of Pandit Ghasiram's house and screams : 'Maharaj, you made him chop wood when he had fever only the other day. He had nothing to eat this morning. He had no strength and you made him work so hard. What harm had he done that you were so cruel?'

Ghasiram and Lakshmi cower in a corner, frightened by the truth. But in their hearts they know that the storm will pass.

Reality: Sarhupur — *The Vultures.*

It is 7.30 at night by the time the village *pradhan* Navinchandra Agarwal, finally musters the courage to do his duty. He understands what this incident means, and he realizes that he will have to get police help immediately if further carnage is to be avoided. He does not use the road, but walking across the fields, he reaches the Makhanpur railway station and telegraphs the Shokohabad police that there has been a massacre of Harijans in his village. The police, as usual, are not exactly brisk in their reactions, and reach the village around 11. Now the wireless begins crackling, and by morning the rest of the world is being told there is a village in India called Sarhupur.

The processions begin arriving that day, the last day of 1981. The police chief, the Minister for Home Affairs of Uttar Pradesh. By one in the afternoon, the Chief Minister himself comes, wearing a very, very long face, and immediately offers blood money: so many thousand rupees per death. And then the factory begins manufacturing lies.

The first priority of the Government is to ensure that the Thakur dacoits are not blamed for this massacre, since the CM is a Thakur and the Thakurs had committed the Dehuli massacre. So, by 3.30 on the afternoon of 31 December, a letter is fabricated by the police: this letter, say the police, is from Anar Singh (the Yadav dacoit) and was left behind by him after he had killed the Harijans. The assailants, therefore, the police say, are Yadavs, not Thakurs. It is such an incompetent fabrication that it is soon exposed. The administration soon shuts up about this theory. Then they try to make political capital out of the tragedy by saying that the massacre was organized by the Opposition in order to defame the CM! In fact the whole effort of the administration now revolves around not trying to find the killers, but towards tarnishing the already dented image of the Opposition. Instead of solutions the search is on for scapegoats: The corpses have become another toy in political games.

Nor is this the attitude of the Government alone. The Opposition too begins its search for votes: Unity talks are to be held at Sarhupur! What a farce! Atal Behari Vajpayee leads a *padayatra* interrupted by car rides to other places: The last leg of the *padaya-*

tra would have been hilarious if it was not so sad. Mr Vajpayee leads a group of bhajan singing followers to mourn the dead with a public meeting. And who is in that group? The moneylenders who haunt these villages, of course. There, for instance, is the *lala* from Makhanpur who has built the walls of his house extra thick to protect his ill-begotten money stolen from the misery of the poor. These are the protectors of the Harijans!

It does not take long for the interest of even the Opposition parties to die. By the end of January, the dead Harijans have been forgotten. The vultures have picked all the flesh from the corpses.

Art: Sadgati — *The Vultures.*

The Chamar's body has begun to stink. Pandit Ghasiram is pacing up and down, thinking. The wailing of the Chamars continues, but not one of them is willing to come to the rescue by taking away the stinking body. It is well past midnight now, and the storm is finally abating. Lakshmi cannot contain her frustration: 'These witches have eaten my brains. Can't they stop crying?' Pandit Ghasiram replies: 'Let these demons weep. How long can they cry?' 'Yes,' Lakshmi points out, 'but the weeping of Chamars is inauspicious, it brings misery.'

Dawn is breaking; the body is still lying there, and now the stink is spreading. The Brahmin mind which Pandit Ghasiram possesses finally finds a solution. He knows now how he will remove the body himself, and without breaking his caste, without being forced to touch the body of the untouchable.

Pandit Ghasiram takes out a rope and makes a noose of it. Using the axe, he forces one of Dukhi's stiff legs up and slips the noose around it and winds it tightly. Then Pandit Ghasiram, a cloth around his nose to keep off the stench, begins pulling the rope and hauling the body away. It is hard work for a man of his sensibilities and physique; he stumbles in the slush and the weight is a heavy burden but he continues to pull, across the field and over the hill, and into the rubble and thorny bushes where Dukhi Chamar finds his final resting place. A relieved Pandit Ghasiram returns home and quickly has a bath to purify himself. Fresh sandalwood marks now adorn his face. He begins mumbling prayers, and takes a mug of holy water which he sprinkles on the spot where Dukhi died:

that too must be purified.

In the sky the vultures are wheeling; they have found their meal for the day. Dukhi Chamar.

February 1982

Death had a Signature

Bihar is at once the richest and the poorest State in India: rich in natural resources, poor in the quality of life it offers its inhabitants. It is also perhaps the most corrupt and the most prone to violence. Dacoit gangs roam the countryside robbing and killing. They are seldom brought to book because few people dare to stand up to them: the police and politicians are often in league with them. This scene is set at Umarchak, a few days after it was raided by such a gang on the night of 15 January 1986.

What happens to an idea when it is thrown into the whirling crucible of reality? A free Government has been functioning since 1947; laws have been enacted to end social oppression; plans have been made to end hunger. But how have those plans and laws percolated down, and what do they end up as? What is the truth about India's villages, and how does this reality respond to notions of progress: after all the term 21st century has a meaning only if understood as a metaphor of progress. To explore these questions it is necessary to go to the poorest villages, deep in the countryside, where life and sudden death impinge but rarely on the world outside.

This report is from a village in Bihar, where on the night of 15 January a gang of dacoits shot five people dead, shouted out their names and went away, confident that the Government was but a mirage slightly over fifty kilometres from the capital.

Statistic: An average of seven dacoities is reported to the police every day in Bihar. The Indian Penal Code defines dacoity thus: 'Robbery is dacoity if the offenders are more than five in number. The gravity of the offence is measured by the terror presumed to be created by the force of numbers.'

Umarchak: This murder story at least needs no detectives. The killers were in fact a little worried that the fear-frozen villagers huddled in their huts, might never be certain who they were if they did not identify themselves. And there would be little point in the murder if it were anonymous: For death to have an impact beyond flesh and bone, a signature had to be placed on every bullet. And so the leader of the gang of dacoit-killers screamed into the night after shooting dead five men: 'I am Jugal Gop. I have taken my revenge, *Jai Mahavir!*'

Thirty years after he had become a dacoit, Jugal Gop had come to kill his neighbours in this small, lost village thrown carelessly on the geography of Bihar. He had his reasons: A traditional family feud; a land dispute which went back fifteen years; but, most important, the old anger nourished by a suspicion that these five dead neighbours had tipped off the police about a dacoity he had committed last Diwali leading to the arrest of his son Arjun and the recovery of the loot. Jugal Gop could have killed them on any day; it was his magnanimity which had kept these men alive; at midnight on 15 January his generosity had come to an end. He was the law. That was the message.

The Bihari villager takes death stoically; after all, there is enough of it around. There is little protection from either man or nature when they get into a vile mood. Sital Prasad showed me what was left of the five lives: a pair of plastic sandals sitting undisturbed on the *takht* (an oblong space cut into the mud wall of the hut at eye level), the blood-splattered *nehali* (blanket) crumpled in a corner of the haystrewn floor on which the men had been sleeping, the hay still stained a reddish brown, the colour of dried blood. Sital Prasad kept insisting that I write his name down and mention it in my report. There was an edge of anxiety in his persistence which made it more than a prurient effort to get mentioned, and I asked why. Because he was next, he said. He had heard that Jugal Gop would now come to get him; he was lucky to have been somewhere else that night. The sudden furore had brought a police picket to the village, but for how long? The affable police inspector who joined our conversation, leaving for the moment the comfort of the *charpoy* laid out in the winter sun, readily agreed. It was silly to think that the police could actually protect anyone. In any case they had managed to reach this village only because this was winter and the *kutcha* (country) road had not melted under the first rain, '*Kamoonikesan kahan hai, sir?*' the policeman said. Then, added with a small laugh, '*Police to etney chalne mein thak jaata hai, naa; chorwa kahan se pakraega? Aap ketta chale the, sir?*' (Where is the communication, sir? Our police get tired after walking on foot; where is the energy to catch thieves? How much did you have to walk to reach here?)'

Peace in Bihar's villages is not the gift of the policeman. Even if he had the will, which is far from certain, he would still not be able to save a life. The infrastructure that defines a modern government simply does not exist; and what parts of it were once constructed by national funds earmarked for progress have (for instance, electricity) collapsed under the moribund weight of crime and inefficiency. The occasional benefit of new achievement trickles down to the landed, say in the form of fertilizer. But this is hardly sufficient to provide the conviction of government and security. In any case, which harvest can compete against the gnawing dread of sudden death?

*

'*Bina sarkar ke Hindustan hawo*' (There is no government in Hindustan). The old man was being deliberately provocative, taunting the young who had brought in their new-fangled ideas about freedom and progress and voting rights. Feudalism he understood. Colonialism he understood. What he was confounded by was lawless democracy. Yes, he had the vote. Yes, he too voted. But he also knew how elections were won. 'What can Rajiv Gandhi do to stop dacoits and *goondas*? Nothing. He wins his elections with their rifles and bullets. Today you can buy a judge for Rs. 10,000. This is what police and justice have come to.' All that the white man promised was law and order; he took his revenue in return, but he delivered protection. Today a son wore a watch on his left hand and robbed his father with his right. What did the son need to know the time for? There was dawn, noon, dusk and night; was it more useful to wash a cow or to know whether it was precisely two minutes past ten?

How can you stop the new world? I asked; a watch measured dimensions beyond the capacity of the old man. In another fifteen years, I reminded him, we would see the 21st century.

'I will tell you what else we will see in fifteen years,' the old man answered tartly. 'We will see murder and death.'

Statistic: Bihar has 67,566 villages. 47,393, or around 70 per cent, do not have a proper road. (Comparative figures for Kerala, Punjab and Haryana are zero percent, one and two percent).

Speed is a primary gauge of development. It takes more than four hours to negotiate the 500 odd kilometres from Patna to Umarchak.

You move out of the big city onto National Highway 30 and on either side stretches rich, fertile land whose only problem is that there is too much underground water. What the villagers want is a drainage system; instead they get all the waste and refuse of the city dumped on to their lands. We are travelling beside the Pun Pun river; and this is the heart of the new Naxalite belt, stretching up to Bhojpur and the Sone river. It is here that the Indian People's Front has its strongholds; and it here that the landlords have created their private army in reply, the Loric Sena, whose leader is a Congress (I) member of the Rajya Sabha who proudly calls himself King Mahendra. This is the Lok Sabha constituency of Barh, represented currently by Prakash Chandra, son of the prince of Bihar's Yadavas, Ram Lakhan Singh Yadav, and slightly more famous for the fact that he was interrupted by the Calcutta police in a brothel while otherwise engaged.

The highway becomes patchy soon enough, and our car has already slowed down considerably by the time we are stalled by a queue of stationary trucks. The front pane of one of them - BHY 4776 - has been shattered by students who tried to flag down the truck for a ride but were ignored. These are students of the Ram Lakhan Singh Yadav College. Mr Yadav's reputation as an educationist may not have spread far and wide, nor may there have been honours from Delhi for this, but there are scores of colleges in the State named after him, built with funds obtained through his influence and meant for the young of his caste. (The privatization of education in Bihar takes many and imaginative forms.) No university need recognize the college, and its degree may be of dubious value in the job market but it does provide the illusion of education, and in any case it leads to a higher value in the dowry market.

There seems to be a growing sense of deterioration with each step away from Patna, the capital, and Patna was not too exciting to begin with. At every stage on the way it is as if we are moving back in time: From neon lights to flickering oil lamps; from sandals and shoes to bare feet; from concrete walls to thatched sides that hardly blunt the cold winds of winter nights; from an approximation of progress to a life which has changed little for centuries; from synthetic cloth to wraps and rags. By the time we reach Harnaut, where we must leave the highway, the sense of regression is complete: Electricity has totally disappeared.

The road we now take is, comparatively, a new one, built in the early eighties, and for an interesting reason. It is here that the now famous village of Belchi is situated, where on 27 May 1977, Harijans were burned to death in the first major atrocity of the Janata Raj, and from where Mrs Indira Gandhi began her journey back to power. Stories about Mrs Gandhi's visit in the monsoon of August 1977 still circulate. There, for instance, we see the temple where Mrs Gandhi stopped for something to eat: someone brought her *puris*, and she refused, insisting that she preferred the simple *roti* of the villagers' normal fare — a gesture which flowered into the slogan: '*Aadhi roti khayenge, Indira wapas layenge!*' (We will eat only half a roti, but bring Indira back) Belchi like Umarchak, is beyond the reach of a car. Mrs Gandhi did the last leg on the back of an elephant. We walk.

We leave the 20th century behind at Koraribaghatila, parking our car at the last outpost of Indian banking, a branch of the Punjab National Bank. In a sense the way to Umarchak really begins here, at the end of the road.

Statistic: Forty-three per cent of the villages in Bihar are electrified. But Bihar has only 2.9 per cent of the nation's installed power capacity and only 1.8 per cent of power generation.

You can get completely lost in the middle of flat land. The feeling is exactly similar to being in the middle of the sea. You are the centre of a semi-circle, the sky arching over your head and meeting the earth on every horizon around you. The paths are endless; you have to walk on the boundaries between fields, and it is impossible to go anywhere without a proper sense of navigation. The centre of this unfathomable upturned bowl shifts with you.

'Who is the biggest landowner of the area?', we asked our guide. A man called Ram Saran, he said, who had perhaps five or six hundred *bighas*. But conversation was stilted; it could hardly be otherwise when walking single file. It was mellow and beautiful, the only sound being the occasional raised voice of a person working in the fields, or the cries of children playing as we passed through a village. One villager we overtook could not resist the temptation of asking if the camera we were carrying was a '*door-been*' (the English magistrate always carried his binoculars). Suddenly we heard a cry: 'Sarkari?' It was an old woman walking towards us from the fields, along with her daughter (a strikingly beautiful young woman who was in turn holding her daughter, a baby, in her arms). She was cutting grass, she told us, when the young son of the landlord came and snatched all the grass she had cut. Yes, it was his land, but it was only grass, and it was her labour, and she did not have any land, didn't she have any right to live? Unable to answer any of her questions, I asked her her name. She looked puzzled, and then even blushed. Her daughter by now could hardly contain her embarrassment at the effrontery of her mother talking to city-slick sahibs like this over as mundane a subject as hunger! 'Are you asking an old woman like me her name,' she exclaimed. 'Yes'. 'Rajpuri,' she said, before her daughter hustled her away.

One or two villagers walking the same cracked, hard mud ridge, sometimes looked curiously at us. 'We are going to Umarchak,' I told one and he immediately pretended he had not heard. Had he not heard of the murder of five men at night? No, no, no; he had heard nothing; he was from another village. Then he laughed as I experienced a little difficulty jumping a soggy patch, and had to hold the guide's hand to hop across: '*Chust pantwa rahe se tani jyada dikkar hola*' (It is a little more difficult if you wear tight trousers).

We turned west at a beautiful, spreading banyan tree in full foliage; a little further came a tree with absolutely no leaves at all; is was small and bare and on a bough sat a blue bird, the *neelkanth*, they said it was called. It was an auspicious sight if you were leaving the village on a long journey. We entered the fields of *makai* (maize) and these were bordered by strong wires. I remarked at this sudden presence of wire fencing. These were the wires which had once brought electricity, Ram Prasad, our guide, said. In the early seventies, this area saw for the first time the magic of electricity. Umarchak was among the famous forty-three per

cent of Bihar's villages which all the books in the Planning Commission note have been blessed with electricity. By the middle of
the same decade — he could not exactly date it, but thought 1976
would be accurate enough — the district had gone completely dark
again. Between the thieves and the bureaucrats, the lights had been
put out. The thieves simply cut the wires to sell; then the greater
theft began. The bureaucrats who were sanctioning and buying the
replacements simply decided that there was no point in going
through the whole process of actually putting up the wires for the
thieves to cut them again. They sold the wires themselves.

The bribocrats flourish in the bribocracy called Bihar.

*

*Statistic: The poverty line is defined as an income of Rs. 60 per
month and a daily intake of 2000 calories: fifty-nine per cent of
Bihar, as compared to the national average of forty per cent lives
below the poverty line.*

Property is theft, we learnt. Bihar, always ready to lend an extra
touch of paradox to any aphorism, might well consider turning the
phrase around: Theft is property. If the first maxim is true of one
half of the diarchy which controls Bihar, the landlord, then the
second sums up the morals and behaviour of the other half, the
bureaucracy.

According to one person who should know, since he has been in
charge of the State's political fortunes but thinks it politic to
maintain his anonymity while talking on this subject to me, there
are seven families who form the feudal elite of Bihar: Dinesh
Kumar Singh, Mul Babu, Sahu Parbatta (of Bhagalpur), the
Sahadev family of Ranchi, Jageswar Hit Singh of Palamau and
Jayaram Giri, who controls the *math* of Bodh Gaya. They are
well-represented in the seats of power.

Dinesh Kumar Singh was expelled from the Congress party in
1976 by Chief Minister Jagannath Mishra because of his proven
benami landholding in Katihar and the erstwhile Kutsala State;
the charge was that he had flouted every norm of the Land Ceiling
Act and that such a landlord was not fit to belong to a party which
espoused the cause of the poor and land reform.

Dinesh Kumar Singh, a proud Thakur, and still as big a land-

lord as ever, is Minister for Food and Supplies in the Congress
Government of Bindeshwari Dubey ruling Bihar in 1986. Sarju
Mishra, the Health Minister, is said to control nearly a thousand
acres in Purnea. Bir Narayan Chand is perhaps the biggest of them
all, controlling perhaps as much as five thousand acres in Purnea.
He is also the father of Madhuri Singh, an honourable Member of
Parliament elected on the Congress ticket. The word
'control' rather than 'own' is used for the simple reason that the
landholding is often *benami* (held under a different name).

But truth does not change because everyone's eyes are turned in
a different direction. Land is power, power over resources, power
over people, power over waves, power over a poor man's life and
death. This translates into power over votes; money quickly
becomes power over administrators; the legitimacy is soon provided by political parties whose first (perhaps sole) aim is to fill
enough party labels in the august House oPeople to provide the
magic fifty-one per cent which brings ministerships — Prime,
Chief, Cabinet, State, Deputy. Land reform can wait another
generation. The poor have waited for so many thousands of years;
is there any specific hurry now?

What happens when money large — fat dollops of it — comes
under the generous head of development and enters the charge of
the bureaucrat or politician who is meant to use it to change the life
of the poor? Let's take an example. For more than a century now,
authority has been trying to turn the Sone river into a blessing: An
estimated Rs.75 lakh will be spent at the very minimum with the
completion of the current canal project. An Indian Administrative
Service officer, successor to the heaven-born doyens of the Indian
Civil Service, who taught administration and morality in the
clouds of Mussoorie, and is still young enough to look forward to
the 21st century (he belongs to the 1962 batch), is at the moment
under judicial custody. He was remanded on 10 January, and a
case has been instituted against him and four officials of the State
cadre for suspicion of defalcation of Rs.36 lakh when they were
posted in the Sone Command Development Area in 1981. V.
Prasad, the concerned IAS officer, was Commissioner and
Chairman for just twenty months before being transferred to the
Board of Revenue. Charges: He made payments to a printing press
which never existed and issued and cashed bogus cheques.

Just as an aside, with nothing to do with this particular case, readers might want to know that a recent controversy over the beleagured Sone concerns Chief Minister Dubey's *samadhi* (daughter's father-in-law) Jagdish Pande who has been the engineer in charge of the project although his only qualification in the subject is a diploma and the law book specifically bars mere diploma holders from being put in charge of such a project.

You want stories in Bihar? No problem. Go to Fatua, a little outside Patna, and developed as a prestige industrial area. Two forlorn factories sit side by side: the Bihar Scooter Factory and the Bihar Tractor Factory project, complete with signs exhorting everyone to fulfil the 20-point programme. The factories are more often closed than open; and the corruption is of a wondrous scale. Have you had a good laugh of late? In any case, get ready. Tyres worth Rs.15 lakh were written off in the tractor factory because, according to the managers, rats ate up the tyres. I kid you not. Even the *durwan* laughed as he repeated the story:
'*Moos tyreway kha gara, sir!*' (The rats ate up the tyres, sir!) Such sheer mismanagement would not be condoned anywhere else, and certainly not in any other Indian capital.

One could go on, but what is the point?

The plans are made in Delhi, and the intentions are all honourable. Every Government tries out honesty and effort first before failure turns the vision sour and the Lords of Expediency, hovering in the wings, waiting for their day, confident that their sort of wisdom will triumph in the end, return to the inner chambers of counsel to replace the young hopefuls being given their transfers. But where is the prospect of going anywhere, 20th century or 21st, the heart burdened with the innocent sorrow of the poor condemned to hunger by a fate no one understands, with a machinery as clogged by the selfishness of the rich as ours is? Bihar alone destroys the national statistics of poverty. Against a national urbanization level of twenty-four per cent, Bihar has only twelve per cent. Rs.29 per capita is spent by the nation on health; Bihar spends Rs.17. Fertilizer consumption: Bihar uses 18.5 kgs per hectare against the national average of 36.6 kgs (forget the thought of a State like Punjab which uses 127.8 kgs). Per capita consumption of sugar: 4.4 kgs in Bihar compared to 7.2 kgs nationwide Per capita rural incomes? Rs.395 in Bihar against Rs. 1627 in Punjab and a national mean of Rs 638. Last, or second last, in everything, except size — size of land, size of population, size of the problem.

But how can this awful dilemma called Bihar be possibly solved without shaking the fundamental roots of the poverty, the holding in land, the control, exploitation and corrupt siphoning off of financial and human resources? Can Rajiv Gandhi sack his own ministers for breaking the law of land ceiling? He need not of course, and hope with reason that the status quo will carry him through the next election. No argument about that. And of course he could always march into the 21st century hand in hand with the Thakurs who dominate thousands of acres: the computers could as easily work out finer margins of exploitation as they could charge the wheels of change — after all computers are mute. Nor is it possible to tinker and imagine that convicting one IAS officer is the miracle whitener which is suddenly going to turn Bihar cleaner than clean. Only one revolution can spring from the soil of Bihar as it is now, and that is not the green one. If poverty has to be tackled, it must begin from the most fundamental base — that of the land and the resources it produces season after season. Those resources can flower, with different ownership and proper management, into industry and development that can bring calories to the lowest of the low, the rat-eaters and the untouchables who have neither land nor any hope of ever getting it. Bihar is rich: its land is golden, its sinews powerful, its minerals vast, its potential dynamic. But its people are poor, its structures are rotten and oiled by the worst decadence. Cynicism, if not outright theft, is the philosophy of the powerful. The smell of hunger and malfeasance fills the air: the world here is controlled by an anti-culture, a cancer which took root many hundreds of years ago and still remains unshaken, although the law of the Constitution will be middle-aged tomorrow and the promise of the new dawn has become the saddest cliche. What will happen to Umarchak, and those 67,565 other villages of Bihar? There will be growth, of course, and the creation of wealth, but who will it go to? Will the child of hunger, born in 1947, die in 2000 without once having met the 20th century?

January 1986

The Spiders of Orissa

Kalahandi in Orissa, once ruled by tribal kings, is now amongst the poorest regions in the country. Most of the land has been bought by outsiders and many of its inhabitants reduced to beggary and prostitution. Deaths by starvation are common, but are stoutly denied by officials of the State Government and other 'vested interests' — the only ones who prosper in this forsaken corner of India.

> As for those three red-faced card players — they are the guards. One smells of garlic, another of beer, but they're not a bad lot. They have wives they are afraid of, kids who are afraid of them; they're bothered by the little day-to-day worries that beset us all. At the same time they are policemen; eternally innocent, no matter what crimes are committed; eternally indifferent, for nothing that happens can matter to them.
>
> From *Antigone* by Jean Anouilh

They don't like it at all when Prime Ministers try and create spaces in the web. The threads by which the tribal has been trapped have taken a long time to weave. To create a good slave you must first kill his pride, his self-respect, his notion of himself as an ordinary, equal human being. The slave's body is needed — the man's for labour, the woman's for labour and abuse; but to control the body the inner spark which ignites anger must be crushed. There are many weapons in the spider's arsenal, both psychological and physical, but the chief one is dramatically simple: hunger. When a generation or two dies of the ultimate denial, delirious for a handful of rice, while a chorus of spiders fattens indifferently in the background, physical and mental slavery becomes an easy option to the dying. The young woman at your feet is not prostrate through love or devotion; she is there because over many lifetimes she has learnt that the degradation of the spirit is the only guarantee she has against the degradation of the body, that food and safety are not her right but a gift which a superior might grant if she behaves. The man, his taut, dark body glistening with a youth which will fast wither, is allowed the hint of a sullen look, but no more. Oppress by destitution. Keep a people on the permanent knife-edge of hunger: normalcy should never mean more than one meal of rice and *dal* a day; and a bad year as is the case this year (1985) in this tribal district of Orissa, should mean wild fruit and *mahua* (a country) liquor till the poison wrecks what is left of the body.

The tyrant is no longer the feudal with a hunting crop, throwing heroic virgins off the parapet for refusing to submit to his evil designs; he is now the red-faced card player, afraid of his wife, who keeps the web tightly meshed. Oppression has been democratized. The police constable, the district official, the small-time middleman, the bank clerk, the new settler: these are the guards over the body of Antigone's brother, preservers of a tyranny that works in their favour, willing to support any change of leader as long as there is no change of system.

They are not rich, either in imagination or in money, but not any the less brutal for that. No one is as vicious towards the destitute as those who might slip into destitution any moment, no one is more contemptuous of the tribals and the Harijans as those whose castes keep them a mere notch inside the touchable pale. In 1951, eighty per cent of the arable land in Kalahandi belonged to tribals; today only twenty per cent does. Settlers from neighbouring Madhya Pradesh and Andhra Pradesh or even faraway Rajasthan bought the tribals out since was no legal protection to the marginal farmer. The Government provides generous loan options on paper; the tribal cannot get the loan because he defaulted the last time. The district official refuses to see the famine in front of him, and passes on this verdict to the State capital where no one wants bad news in any case. And so, despite being the worst affected district in Orissa, Kalahandi gets much less relief than Bhubaneswar or Cuttack. When Bhakti Roy, the lean twenty-seven-year-old MLA from the district, warned of the famine in the summer session of the State Assembly, the answer he got was a bland denial. What famine? Where? Kalahandi? That is normal hunger, friend, not a famine;

nobody is dying — you opposition members always exaggerate. Roy threw a microphone, but it takes more than a flying missile to disturb the equanimity of a minister. In the same tradition of convenient eyesight, no famine deaths have taken place so far in Kalahandi. The Government's record is clean. Close your eyes and the truth will cease to exist. Particularly the truth about tribals. If some stray hack picks up the story and writes it, ignore that too. Twenty-four hours later no one will bother. The world is too busy trying to survive.

The real trick is to destroy the confidence of a people: make them believe the caricatures you have created about them. Less than 500 years ago, these tribals of Orissa and Bastar and Andhra ruled over a brilliant empire; today they have been turned into parodies of a cruel fiction. The tribal man is a *mahua*-swigging drunk. The woman is an easy lay. The strength of this hoax lies, of course, in the fact that it is constructed on a malicious distortion of reality to give it the facade of believability. The tribal does like a drink and has none of the hypocritical duplicity of the middle class towards liquor. That does not make him a drunkard. The woman is beautiful; she does not wear a blouse and no one in her village looks twice at her exposed breast; leering is the prerogative of the starved visitor. To equate this with prostitution is the task of the pervert. What has made one tribal an emaciated drunkard and another a prostitute in Raipur or Bilaspur or Calcutta is hunger; gnawing, tearing, shattering hunger. And the last stage of hunger: despair. There is no hope left of escaping from the web, so lie somnolescent at its centre, praying that destiny grants you a few extra days before the spider inevitably consumes you.

A Prime Minister's visit to a tribal village stirs this web, and the silken strands bend and blow open as they might in a passing breeze, creating the illusion that the web is about to break. The spider becomes uneasy. The victim begins to wonder. Then comes the dangerous moment: the quiet, half-hidden, hesitant gleam in the eye. Hope. Is someone by any chance showing an escape route from the web? Why is such a busy and important man coming to a village in Kalahandi after ferrying across two rivers in monsoon rage? In that slime of placid, undisturbed despair, stirs an old embryo: hope.

But the spiders know about this too. They have seen it all before.

The last time there was a big to-do about famine in Kalahandi, Mrs Indira Gandhi herself came, just like her son, in the early days of her Prime Ministership. Irrigation, she said, was the only way out as only four per cent of the land was assured of water; irrigation would increase productivity, provide two crops a year, give the landless work and rescue the tribal from the downward spiral. The spiders nodded. Plans for two major projects were made. Schemes drawn up. Money sanctioned. Nothing very much happened after that. Except of course that the spiders have calmly consumed what they could digest of the projects. No, it is not only the evil Congress which has kept the tribals where they are; even the beatific parties of the opposition have done their bit. (Opposition parties of every hue have taken their turn at Government in Bhubaneswar since the Sixties.) Spiders do not belong to political parties; political parties belong to them.

Once again a Prime Minister has disturbed them; this time, worse, a youngish one, who seemed to convey a personal degree of sympathy when he came in the heat of July. A little difficult, but not beyond the grinding abilities of the spiders. They had tackled the grandfather, after all, and he used to be, with all that rhetoric about socialism, a bit of a handful. Even Raj Kapoor and Dev Anand had hope in those days just after freedom. Remember that line from the slick boy-meets-underworld-thriller *Kala Bazaar*? The khadi-clad social worker finds a derelict in a park, picks him up, and, in a comment on his own penury as well as the derelict's, says, 'Now freedom has come. Now at least the doctors will not charge anything to see a patient.' That was the hope of the Fifties. The spiders made you wait in queues outside charitable dispensaries and charged bribes to take you up the line by the time Jawaharlal Nehru died.

And the same game goes on. For the benefit of the Prime Minister (who, of course, is keen about the follow-up measures) meetings are called in a hurry and end in a flurry. A great show of generosity is put up. The slow process of disinformation then begins (the close friends of the spiders, the flies who wallow in the parlour, we journalists, are ever obliging). Things are not really that bad. The girl who you thought had been sold for forty rupees is actually happily married. You know poor people, they tend to dramatize things in front of the Prime Minister. This is a poor country anyway: what do you expect the people to eat — apples? The rains have come, and one good shower in September will ensure a bumper crop this year. What about the irrigation projects? Where's the money? Don't get taken in by passing dramatics: thank you very much and goodbye, hope to see you when the Prime Minister comes to inaugurate a steel plant rather than to see starving tribals.

One day soon the queries from the Prime Minister's Secretariat will dry up as more monumental challenges occupy Delhi's attentions. The passing breeze will have been harnessed. The world will become normal again.

Ever tried exterminating spiders? Difficult. Particularly when they are so very good at cleaning up the debris of hope.

September 1985

Revelations Down South

In southern India today, untouchables enjoy a few more privileges than before, in large measure due to the battles fought to end caste discrimination by people like E.V Ramaswamy Naicker (Periyar) and Baba Sahab Ambedkar. But discrimination still has its corrosive subtleties.

His personality took shape in stages. But perhaps it would be more sensible to report where, before who, since the leader is a child less of his parents than of his circumstances.

Peria simply means big. A visitor hearing the name of this colony for the first time might be forgiven for assuming that it is named after 'Periyar' E. V Ramaswamy Naicker, the founder of the Dravida movement who tried to create a lower caste-untouchable alliance in his effort to break the stronghold of the Brahmin, but the suggestion is laughed away by the Harijans who live here. They have no illusions about either father Naicker or his children, the three Dravida parties (The All India Anna Dravida Munnetra Kazhagam — AIDMK — led until 1987 by the late M.G. Ramachandran the DMK led by K. Karunanidhi, and the original, now nominal, faction of the movement still loyal to 'Periyar') curently operating in Tamil Nadu — one in power, one in the opposition, and one in an advanced stage of inertia. They would ideally like their colony to be named after the one authentic national Harijan hero, Babasaheb Ambedkar, but that would mean another fight with the caste Hindus, and life is difficult enough as it is. In fact, the one real road running through this sprawling Harijan colony is called the Govind Raja Perumal Street after the grandfather of a local Naidu luminary, and that does not particularly please anyone either, but there are more things to confront the municipality with than the names of streets. Those inclined towards searching for symbolism might find a better harvest in the fact that Peria Colony is bound by Mahatma Gandhi Road to the east, Pandit Jawaharlal Nehru Road to the south, and Kamaraj street to the north. And when the combined weight of three pious legacies fails to save them from violence, the Harijans can always turn west to Hospital Road, so named because of the Government hospital there. But it is the memory of Gandhi and the work of Kamaraj which has kept the Harijans not only in Peria Colony but all over the State firmly committed to the Congress. Gandhi raised the historic slogan and gave them a visionary identity: The children of Hari Kamaraj, after he took away power from the arrogant Brahmin lobby within the State Congress and became Chief Minister, gave them protection and food. The first noon-meal scheme for children was started by Kamaraj and for Harijans only.

Peria is at the eastern end (where else could it be?) of Villupuram town, opposite the main bus stand and the market. But once you turn in from the main road—a typical complex of small shops serving small needs: selling lottery tickets, bananas, magazines, tea, savouries, the loud cassette player of the teashop once again destroying the local language voodoo, *Laila O Laila* blaring away with a passion that only Hindi films seem to be able to generate in every corner of united India—you enter a different world. At one level it is the same: Lottery tickets are needed here as much as on the main road, and perhaps more. So are teashops. The women crowded around the municipal watertap could by anywhere, chattering as they wait their turn, the younger girls forming their own groups, their pretty smiles waiting to age with the first child, the first brawl with a drunk husband, the first touch of reality or responsibility or whatever you want to name the disillusionment of adulthood. The children, dark and dirty and vociferously embarked upon their two principal activities, laughing or crying, would be the same in any slum. The huts are thatched and brown, with only the very occasional small brick house recognizing the presence of marginal upward mobility. Normal. But it is this very normalcy which is the news.

These people, once they reach the main street, once they leave this colony to do whatever they do for a living — pull a rickshaw, carry a load on their back (a rupee for a legitimate burden, something extra if they are taking smuggled or stolen goods to a shop in the market), sell vegetables, pimp, prostitute themselves, carry distilled country liquor — do anything which brings them into contact with the world of caste Hindus and Muslims, then they become different, they become members of a race so cruelly punished by misfortune that they become lower than animals, then the only touch they know from other human beings is the powerful and vicious touch of exploitation, plunder of body and esteem. On the main road is scorn and hate or at best patronizing liberalism. Here, on this patch of land in the east, they can live out their quota of joy, sorrow, anger, boredom, health, disease, indulge their distinct habits. Without fear, the untouchables can touch each other.

*

The first thing we saw as we entered Peria Colony was the carcass of a cow or a buffalo being cut up — in all probability the animal had reached the Harijans dead, it would be simply too valuable alive for them to afford it. The meat was being handed out and accepted with relish. We strolled down the Raja Perumal Street. Inevitably eyes turned towards us city slickers. A middle-aged woman, very self-possessed, turned to my friend (he had come along to translate) and asked whether we had come to buy a cow. She was surprised when we said no. Why else should one of us come here? A few of them raised cattle, and the price of a calf or milch cow was often cheaper here, as it would always be in the case of a seller without holding power. Who else could we be? Not police officers. They wouldn't come so early in the morning, to begin with and not alone: A single policeman is a policeman without status, and we can't have that, can we? Nor had there been any hint of trouble. There had been no fight last night between the two gangs. And no one had heard of one of the girls being molested or raped by the caste Hindu loafers who hung around on the outskirts of Peria when returning from the cinema. Nor was there trouble with the prostitutes, everyone knew that Nattar was virtually running a brothel, but he paid the constables on time and never created any trouble, at least as long as the customers paid the pimps the negotiated amount. The criminal fringe was only understandable in a colony like this one: in any case, they were needed.

Who else would provide the protection when the caste Hindus attacked? If there had been peace after the great riot of 1978, it had been thanks partly to the gangs. The last thing you do in a three-paisa opera is impose middle-class morality. Mac the knife could well be your local political bigwig. How would you class the municipal councillor Loganathan? Judges had called him a criminal, and there were cases against him but would they have pursued him if he had not been a Harijan, had not stood up for their rights? And who could forget what he had done in July 1978, during the riots which broke out when that Vanniya Kaliamurthi, who used to work in a vegetable stall, had grabbed the breasts of Salammal in front of everyone? What could Salammal's husband Shanmugam do except beat him up when he learnt about the incident? Why blame him for everything that happened later? On yes, Salammal wasn't sin-free, everyone knew that too, but that did not give Kaliamurthi the right to stare at her all the time, and that too in front of everyone! *Chee*! The only good thing that could be said about the riots that followed was that the caste Hindus didn't get away easily. Yes, fourteen Harijans were killed, but the huts of Vanniyas were also burnt in retaliation. She could not remember any other occasion when, if ever, Harijans had retaliated.

Well, at least it bought a modicum of future peace. All over the district, Harijans — partly inspired by the Ambedkar People's Movement — responding to the new consciousness, having crossed that first barrier of hunger (no movement can begin if your stomach is totally at the mercy of the oppressor) had begun to make their presence felt and the caste Hindus had retaliated, determined to stop a wave which could wash away the terror that held the landlord-labour exploitation in place. In 1978, five Harijans were killed in Ramanathapuram as they tried to force their way into a temple, in 1980, seventeen women were raped and and one man murdered by caste Hindus angered by political protest in Tirunelveli, and so on and on and on, a single rape here, a murder there...

'Take me to your leader,' I said.

His teenage secretary sat at a small wooden desk in the narrow verandah between the protective grille and the proper walls which formed the rooms in which the family lived. Above and to the right was a bank of switches, from the left a staircase rose to the upper floor. Next to the door was the image of Ayyanar, the green and thick-lipped protector who wards off evil. An electric fan was switched on for our elitist needs, as the secretary left the Tamil newspaper he was idling over to take the message of our presence. The leader did not seem properly awake at eight in the morning judging by the time he took to emerge, but maybe he had been kept awake late the previous night serving the people.

He looked at us warily, uncertain of why sahibs would want to come to Peria. He was dark and swarthy, and the flesh hung about parts of his body in mobile if friendly lumps. His dhoti was secure, but the white shirt had been draped loosely. He buttoned it slowly as he made sure of my intentions through the interpreter. The beard was wispy and curling, not a beard so much as a few careless days without a shave.

The hair was thick and ruffled, and the just-awake look extended to his eyes. The conversation had gone some way before his secretary brought his gold-coloured (dial and strap) watch and passed it to him. Without taking his eyes off us, he slipped on his watch.

He was finally fully dressed.

He had built his house only last year, he said, and with some pride pointed out that every important political leader of Villupuram, including the MLA, had come for the opening ceremony. Where had the money come from for this house? He lowered his eyes modestly, 'I don't smoke... I don't drink... I worked hard... I took a bank loan... The others drink their money away... I saved... and built my house at last... 'Perhaps he paused regularly out of habit. For applause.

He sent for and proudly showed us his identity card. P. Chellam was staff number 554 and the card was valid till 31 December 1986.

He had the qualities necessary to make a politician: a growing confidence in himself which gradually outpaced his weaknesses, an ability to move upward (hut to fan to transistor to cows to house) and, therefore, become a role model, a good understanding of the forces that constructed and protected the society of the poor, and better still, a knowledge of how best to put them to more productive purpose, a plasticine morality which helped him ignore what expediency if not conscience told him to ignore, and most important, a genuine desire to use what was available, both legitimate and illegitimate, for the good of the people he continued to live near. Often, in our pervasive cynicism about politicians, we forget that there is this function which a politician does perform. Last, he was never short of answers: an extremely useful attribute to those who must live by the people.

Could his party, the Congress, ever come to power in his State? 'No problem. We defeat ADMK also. But groups! Tch,tch, tch, Subramaniam one side,Maragatham Chandrashekhar one side, Moopanar one side... Tch, tch, tch.' The clucking was soft but very audible. 'And then Shivaji Ganesan. Law to himself.'

He wanted to become an MLA: that was his ambition. Given a reasonable turn of the cards, he might even become one. He had one purpose: to defeat or defuse the DMK, in his view, the real oppressors of Harijans. The Harijans of the Congress were now allies, they had lost their large land holdings because of the land reforms, and the new owners, the middle castes, had become the new oppressors. And they were the worst, they had none of the saving graces of feudalism and all the viciousness of the nouveau riche. And the worst of them all were the Gaundas, he said, the caste just within the pale. They were cultivators and made the Harijans work on the land like animals. Who got the Government-approved eleven rupees a day? No one. 'Go to the villages,' he said. 'Go and see what they are doing to us — here they may come in the night sometimes and burn us. The law is always supporting these people. And there is anonymity in murder by fire. They can kill while we're sleeping... tch... tch... but there the death is slow, it comes drip by drip every day. On the fields, in the community centre. A Harijan child can't eat at the noon-meal centre with the others. Go to Sannakunam and meet Kaliyanvaradan. Go to Gudalur where Rajendran lives. They will tell you.'

*

In Sannakunam east is east and west in west, and never the twain shall meet.

Kaliyanvaradan has been transferred fifteen times during the thirteen years he has been a teacher at the Panchayat Union Middle School at Sannakunam. The Rs.750 he got every month made him well-to-do in his community. There were cows in a proper stable in front of his hut, and a curved pipe with a bulb at the end over the thatched roof announced the presence of electricity. He brought out a plastic, folding bed for me to sit on, it was an efficient replacement for the *charpoy*. The reason why he was constantly being transferred (thankfully they could not by regulation, send him out of the district) was simple: he had dared to organize the Harijans and challenge the power of the Mudaliars. But of course Kaliyanvaradan was lucky. Not too long ago he would have been simply killed and the body thrown into some shrubbery. Salavan Noran reminded him.

They had all clustered, old men, old women, the young, children, watching with a variety of expressions this man with a notebook and pen asking about their life. Nobody would sit on the plastic cot with me; the teachers preferred to stand, as did most of the others; a few old people sat on their haunches on the ground. Noran was one of them, a tall walking stick resting in one hand, the dark face furrowed, eyes almost shut and peering upwards. He was startled and answered with a blank face when I asked him his age. When the question registered, he replied with a gesture which said, how do I know, I just know that I am very old. He had been a labourer all his life, the two acres he had inherited never seemed enough to sustain the family. Yes, he remembered the old days, and the others, particularly the young, kept encouraging his memory. They were not allowed to wear a *dhoti*, he recalled, all they were allowed to keep on was a piece of cloth called a *kovanam*. This was nothing but a short, oblong piece of coarse cotton, covering the front and the back — the indignity of nakedness was a confirmation of contempt, another message that the untouchable was not going to be allowed an identity, which naturally would be the first step to self-respect. Once he began to respect himself, how could he accept the passive role of the oppressed? No, said Noran, they were not allowed to wear any footwear. They could not ride a bullock cart. Suddenly the old man got animated, as if the memory had hurt him in particular: they were not allowed to see the social drama at the temple, and I could see in his half-closed eyes the hurt of a child longing to see that drama, perhaps crying to see it, fantasizing about it, dreaming about it and when finally the time did come when he could see a drama, his eyes had given out, instead of the hero and heroine all he could see was a blur. They could not drink the water of the village well, and had to use a dirty, muddy pond for all their needs on their side of the village.

I turned to an old woman with small, round spectacles which she had got free from a Government dispensary two years ago. She obviously liked jewellery because she had on a metal necklace and six rings on her fingers. Women could not eat on a plate, she remembered, only on their hands. When they went to work in a caste Hindu's house, they used a separate path at the back, and then ensured that they cleaned the dirt without polluting any family member. The punishment for the slightest mistake, and no mistake could be more punishable than arrogance, or the least hint of challenge — was either a whip or the stick. Pattamma had been beaten often. Kaliyan, this young man so concerned about rights, would not have had a chance.

The Harijans had always lived on the eastern side of the village, the west was reserved for the caste Hindus. The western side was considered the superior side, and no Harijan could live there. An interesting notion, and perhaps it explains something about our psyche and our attitude towards the West. But the room where the free lunch was available to children under the noon-meal scheme of the Tamil Nadu Government was on the western side in Sannakunam village, and the Harijan children had to go there to eat since the Government formally did not recognize discrimination. And that created the problem. The Mudaliars would not allow the Harijan children to sit with theirs. They were not only made to sit outside, but given the leftovers after the caste children had had their fill. Kaliyanvaradan objected. The tension got worse when a young Harijan widow Katai, was appointed to help Mangayar Karsi, the caste Hindu woman in charge. The Mudaliars and Udaiyars seethed at the thought of a Harijan in the kitchen, and withdrew their children from the scheme as long as she was allowed into the kitchen.

On 19 February last year came Shivratri. By tradition sand and clay is collected from the burning ground by the Harijans and given to the priest at the temple of Angalamman. (Why does this happen? Because it has always happened. After the *puja*, the image of Shiva is broken and the dust is distributed as *vibhuti*, first naturally to the caste Hindus and later also to the Harijans). Last year, instead of being given *vibhuti*, the Harijans were attacked by a crowd of caste Hindus armed with *trishuls*. They were taking their revenge for the temerity of the Harijans during the noon lunch. Seven men and three women went to hospital. A hut was set afire. The police came only around midnight, and then took what was neatly described as a 'compromise' statement. The next morning, despite the presence of the law, the Harijans were attacked again. After that there was peace, and the administrative wheels took over to restore 'harmony.' Harijans were arrested, while Mudaliars remained unaffected. Katai was not allowed to cook anymore, so the successful noon-meal scheme of the Chief Minister of Tamil Nadu continued to be successful: the caste children ate inside the room and the Harijans in the open. A caste Hindu woman was appointed to help Mangayar Karsi, and Katai earned her salary by sweeping the floor, which all the Mudaliars were agreed fitted her status. Sannakunam was normal once again.

Kaliyanvaradan looked at me at the end of his story, his face betraying the excitement of yet another act of revenge (he had told a journalist of the English-speaking world his story!) and helplessness. I began to feel guilty. He truly thought that I with my notebook and typewriter could *actually* do something. It made me feel a little ashamed, like another exploiter, using this brave school teacher whom, most probably, I would never see again, to get my story and go home.

But he had still another story to tell, and took me to the neighbouring village of Ayandur Gudalur, two kilometres away, which had the distinction of having the most prosperous Harijans in the region which would certainly make them best-off in the country, since Tamil Nadu's Harijans are a hundred times better off than, say, Bihar's (In fact, the reason why I went there was to see what life was like for the top-of-the-scale untouchable.) The richest of them all owned as much as forty acres of land, and almost three quarters of the 1,000 odd Harijan population owned land. There were twenty boys in high school and ten in college. And, incidentally, the noon meal centre was in the east, the Harijan side, in this village. So the caste Hindu children just did not come there. (Perhaps all the meal centres should be in the east. Hunger would be a reasonable challenge to untouchability.)

*

Young Rajendran's father should never have bought the tractor. It stood proudly in front of their house, like a prize bull, its forehead decorated with paper flowers just as a favourite bull might be adorned with flowers each day. The house was built in 1957, and on the walls of the porch were three pictures of Kamaraj, whose name is still magic to the Harijans. The tractor, TNF 6310, came in 1980 with the help of a State Bank of India (Bharat State Bank they called it) loan. That was when the caste Hindus couldn't take it anymore. They had already been irritated when Rajendran, as a student in the Villupuram Arts College, stood for election, and despite their campaign against him, won. When victorious he came to the nearby Ayandur railway station, they beat him up. It was a reminder to the upstart, telling him who was still in charge of the village no matter what bouquets he may have received in college. Then, thanks to the weightage given to Harijans by Government agencies, Rajendran got the kerosene dealership for the area of Hindustan Petroleum.

The last straw came when prohibition was lifted in Tamil Nadu : Rajendran obtained a licence for an *arrack* (country liquor) shop. Boycott and abuse were the weapons of the caste Hindus. They preferred to go kilometres away to Manbalapattu or Mogaiyar for their *arrack*, and on the way back they would make it a point to create some trouble near Rajendran's shop. One day they attacked the shop. The police, determined to be 'balanced', arrested people from both communities, but only the cases against the Harijans seemed to get pursued (the Sessions Court later just threw the cases out). That was when Rajendran gave up. The licence went to a caste Hindu.

Rajendran is the dilemma. He is stretching the patience of even his friends, forget the mass ranged against him out of prejudice: even his friends are beginning to wonder why he should be the beneficiary of reservations and sundry other benefits. The arguments are all coming out, some of them sophisticated. Why should the privileged Harijan get advantages? No one questions the inbuilt privileges that other communities have got, thanks to an inequity that has continued for centuries, but a few successful Harijans seem to bring out deep and even unknown reserves of hostility, and even the most liberal mind gets a little cynical.

The evidence is produced : have you seen how much untouchability there is among untouchables, between one another ? It becomes fashionable to claim that the Harijan is the true winner of Indian liberalism, all because one airhostess from the 'reserved' quota did not live up to the sophisticated standards of Mr Passenger, all because one boy with eighty per cent marks did not get into a.medical college while the Harijan with pass marks was allowed. As if centuries of inequality could be·suddenly straightened out in the space of three decades which have seen far less change than has been claimed.

In Bihar they are worse off even than the tribals, according to a Home Ministry report. In the first six months of last year in Madhya Pradesh, 4,007 crimes against Harijans were recorded : given that police statistics indicate only less than a single digit percentage of the truth, the figure is appalling. But there are no agitations about this. Anti-reservation wars, on the other hand, can rock a State. And how often does anyone get convicted for atrocities against Harijans? In one of the most famous cases, where forty-two women and children were burnt to death in Kilvenmani in December 1968, and a village turned to ashes, the High Court of Madras acquitted all the accused since the

'intrinsic infirmities' of the evidence made it impossible to pass sentence. The High Court was of the learned view that those who had set fire to the huts had no knowledge that forty-two people were trapped inside. Newspaper reports had said that those men, women and children were deliberately locked into one hut which was then torched. The landlords had marched to that village armed with guns. Evidence is a chimera, but the burnt heart, the darkened mind is a reality. The High Court thought it thoroughly improbable that landlords would personally come to commit such arson and murder. Wouldn't they simply send their servants instead? Good thinking!

Before 1931, the scheduled castes were called depressed or exterior. The British, wanting to enumerate, decided the norms for determination of untouchables. Nine questions were framed : could X be served by a Brahmin? Could X be served by tailors, barbers, water carriers etc who also served caste Hindus? Did X pollute a higher caste by contact? Could X serve water which would be accepted? Could X use public services without a problem? Could X enter a temple? Would X be treated as an equal by caste men even if he had the same educational qualifications? Was X depressed because of his ignorance or, lastly, whether it was because of occupation and birth? The term depressed was changed in 1935 by a special order of the Government of India. But how much of the depression has really gone, and how much is yet to go?

An urban collective protecting its gains with a rough-and-ready lumpen fringe, much weaker than its parallels elsewhere, but at least for the first time ready to fight; A political leadership which is ambitious: in these circumstances a driver's job is sufficient to be a springboard, and a sprinkling of English words, picked up from the sahib's leftover conversations, can be a great asset. The ways of escape from the spit and grovel of the Harijan's existence are hard, and often the escape is to nothing more than the lower reaches of the national income. The authentic, emerging catalysts are under pressure. In the first two decades after independence they were helped up by others, today they spend their time protecting the limited gains of the past thirty years, wondering how much longer the patience of the liberal will last, when the propaganda will find a response in legislative circles. They need a mixture of cunning and bravery to survive, holding the ladder of success with one hand and a despairing brother with the other. One day, perhaps, the structure that is being so patchily constructed may become honestly habitable.

In the mean time, shout if need be, shut up if life hangs by just the thread of silence. Survive. Survive first. The rest comes later. After all, you are whatever little you are today because of one decisive moment of history created by one naked fakir. It is a slice of luck. You may so easily have been your father.

February 1986

The Land of Seven Hundred Hills

A sizeable proportion of India's population consists of Adivasis (aboriginals) who still live in the jungles. These children of the forest had little contact with urban civilization until various groups of people — timber contractors,missionaries, government functionaries — came looking for them, each with its own motives. Today the tribals have begun to fight back.

Saranda Forest: Our guard of honour is made up of five small blue and yellow birds. They appear just a little after we enter the forest. They are sitting on the road when we near them and then for quite a while they fly in front of our car, hopping back on to the ground when they go too far ahead, and then again flitting through the air ahead of us as we catch up. A peacock, disturbed while pecking for food, looks up, pauses a little, and then walks away with quiet dignity. The dry, brown, crumbling leaves crunch with a loud crackling sound under the wheels, disturbed for the first time perhaps since they have fallen from the sal trees: not much traffic passes this way. The silence is broken by a noisy waterfall. It is getting dry now, with the onset of winter, but in the monsoon the hills echo and reecho with the song of tumbling water. The evening sun sparkles through the branches of the tall sal trees. We are in the heart of Asia's biggest sal forest, Saranda, the Land of Seven Hundred Hills, and the protected home of the tribals.

Earlier on in the journey, a tree trunk slung across the road, and then locked to a stump, had stopped us at the edge of the forest, and we had to show our written permission before we were allowed in. *Nature's loveliest poem Is A Tree and Tree Plantation Combines The Goodness Of All Religions* — different ideas merged into single sentences by some poetic bureaucrat and painted on boards for public nourishment. These had become victims of time and lay broken in a corner. The caretaker at the barrier had smiled in relief at the written note from the sahib (he had got word of our imminent arrival, but there was no guarantee like the written word), informed us that he had heard from a truckdriver that one kutcha bridge had broken along the way, and wished us luck on our thirty-kilometre trip to the Kholkabad forest bungalow in the centre of seven hundred hills draped with the graceful sal.

The sal is the tree or life, the sustainer. Its seed is medicine and revenue; it cures dysentery, the killer disease; and when converted into fat it is sold to big factories which, among other things, produce Cadbury's chocolates with its help. The sal is the tribal's spirit and culture. When the Government once tried to develop teak plantations in the forest, the tribals protested, and one day, men from about twenty villages gathered and simply devastated every tree in the area where teak had been sown. Broken trunks piled one upon the other in a sudden clearing in the jungle bore testimony to tribal anger and tribal veneration of nature's loveliest poem. The high point of the year for the tribal is the festival of Sarhul in spring, when the sal flowers; the festival must be held before the first touch of rain falls on the flowers and the date is determined by those who understand the sky. This year (1986), the tribal weathermen have determined that Sarhul will be early, before the end of February.

*

When the administration mounted its last campaign against her, among the things they accused her of was working with the CIA to destabilize India and create a country of the tribals, Kolhanistan. If such indeed are her motives, then Jyotsna has disguised them well. On the walls of her office it might have been reasonable to expect pictures of Jesus Christ and the Pope, in respect of the faith she was born into, or perhaps Queen Elizabeth, in honour of the land which gave her part of her education, and her teenage sustenance. Instead, there are large portraits of V. I. Lenin and Karl Marx.

Perhaps the best thing about her personality is that she is free of the ultimate sin of the reformer — pomposity. She takes her work seriously, not herself. She was born a Syrian Catholic in a small town in Alleppey, Kerala — Kuttanad. 'On the seventh day they baptize you with happiness and joy,' she says with a wry smile that suggests that one's options at that age tend to be somewhat limited. The family was devoted to the Church, and early in her teens she decided to become a celibate and dedicate her life to the service of the poor. 'I would work for the poor, at least as I understood it then.' Instinctively she thought of Bihar; after all, poverty and Bihar have been synonymous for some time. 'We used to learn about Bihar through mission Sundays, when collections would be made; we began to believe that the poor only lived in the north, not Kerala.' A short laugh. 'I was fifteen or sixteen when I decided to join the Notre Dame mission.' She was sent to Britain to be a help to the delegation there. She learnt catering in Northumberland, and then taught in Liverpool. But it was not the poor of England she was going to dedicate her life to. After nine years she came back to Bihar, and started teaching in Patna. This was now 1970.

The mission school was useless, she says; it only concentrated on teaching the children of the elite, who in turn were only interested in learning how to eventually go abroad. She tried to awaken the consciousness of the children by taking them to visit slums, but everyone protested: the children did not want to go there, their parents were shocked, and the school administration angry. The school was happy to let her and four or five friends with similar ideas go. After three months, Jyotsna took leave of absence from the mission and went to live in a tribal village called Sonya near Chakradharpur. She was nervous and afraid, she recalls. But the people accepted her with love. The moment her leave of absence was over she resigned from the mission and continued her individual work. 'I had no longer any fear. I was living with the people.'

Did she turn against the Church? 'Just then I was not taking a position against the Church. The Second Vatican had given hope, and I thought things would change. I had become anti-institution but not yet anti-Church . . . Later I discovered that the Church was itself anti-poor. The students of St. Xavier's Church did not want to disturb the status quo. I lost whatever faith I had in the Church, or in any kind of institution for that matter.'

But not the institution of marriage? I point to the simple gold ring on her finger. 'Oh that! When we were in the Church, we used to wear a silver ring, so I put on a gold one after we left... And you know when you go back home to Kerala they feel a woman must wear some ornament. And I am married now. Raj and I had been working together for so long, I felt, why not get married!' The laughter tinkles across the courtyard.

*

You pays your money and makes your choice. Singbhum derives its name from the Singh Rajas of Porahat who ruled the tribals, says one version, hence the *bhumi* (land) of Singhs. The second interpretation says Singhbhum is a corruption of Singh Ponga, the main god or spirit of the tribals of the district. The Singhs came over from Orissa to rule this neighbouring district through the classical syndrome — tribal jealousies led to division, and anger led to an invitation to the neighbouring feudal who soon took over every village. There are more than fourteen lakh tribals now living in this forest-and-hill-strewn district; not even one-fourth of the more than four-and-a-half-thousand villages have drinking water; and only 218 villages have electricity (thanks to their proximity to mining centres). The only real variation is in the levels of poverty. Get your measuring rod and find who is how far below the line. There are some who still live in the trees. *Birhor* literally means man of the jungle. About a hundred people of this tribe have been settled, thanks to the Tata Steel Rural Development Society, in a small colony about twenty miles from Jamshedpur, but most of them still live in the trees or in rudimentary huts that barely last a rainy season. Life determines what we become most proficient in. They make their huts out of leaves, and their skill is such that if a roof leaks then the man who has made the hut is excommunicated for a month. He must show that he can build a perfect roof of leaves before he is allowed in society again.

*

The dam on the Koyna river catches the water in a pretty valley tucked in the middle of rising, wooded hills. The sun is just above the curving line of trees on the slope, mellow and tired after a long day's work. The sun — the single source of light —shapes the nature of the day. The moon and the stars and the kerosene lamp provide just enough light for a drink of rice wine, song, dance or a last conversation with a friend before it is time to sleep. As the sunlight thins and the cold breeze picks up, the women, as usual harder working than the men, begin the walk back home with bundles of *kundi* leaves on their heads, the result of a full day's work. They have been brought here to the middle of the jungle from Manoharpur by the contractor, to pick these large *kundi* leaves. After the leaves have been dried and the weight of the moisture has evaporated, these leaves will be weighed and the women paid one rupee for every kilogram they have plucked. The money spent on the food they are given is deducted. They have pitched camp on open space beside a running brook; and built huts of leaves.

Public Carrier MPA 6581 is standing there when we reach, ready to take some women back to Manoharpur and perhaps replace them with others for the next day's work. The contractor's name, we learn, is Iqbal Hussein, and these leaves will eventually reach Madras where they will become plates on which food will be served. Who says we are not a secular country: a tribal picks the leaf and is exploited by a Muslim so that a Madrasi Brahmin may eat his vegetarian lunch in pristine purity!

Is one rupee per kilogram (less the money on the food) an average rate? No, even Orissa, not particularly famous for its benevolence towards tribals, has raised the wages for the same work to one-and-a-half rupees per kilogram. Why could not Bihar do it too? Ministers decide these things . . . There are committees. And is it really wise, the man in power tells me, to suddenly raise wages so steeply? Might it not hurt the trade?

Fifty paise may be just a cup of tea in Calcutta or Bombay or Delhi; in the jungle it is a fifty per cent rise in wages. But where is the Government in Bihar to whom the woman plucking the leaves is more important than the contractor?

*

The Civil Procedure Code does not apply in tribal Singhbhum; it is still governed by the Wilkinson Rules. When the British finally subdued the Kohl tribals' revolt in 1832, the man sent to ensure future peace was Captain Wilkinson, and he guaranteed the tribals that their way of life would be protected, that their systems of independent governance would be retained. So it is still.

The first proper administrator to rule from Chaibasa came, in fact, only in 1850. Lt J.S.Davis, a junior assistant agent to the Governor General, was given the job. The position gradually grew in importance. The second District Commissioner was Lt.J.C.Haughton, a principal assistant rather than a junior assistant. By the ninth DC it was a Lt.Col who was the chair, and by the twelfth a full Colonel. The Indian Civil Service proper came only with the arrival of the Right Honourable T.H. Renny on 8 November 1887, and the first Indian as late as in 1906 when Hira Lal Sen, a deputy magistrate, was put in charge, followed by Maulvi Saiyed Karam Husein in 1907 and Hira Lal Banerjee in the same year. The first Indian ICS was B.C. Sen who was posted here in 1913. And then we have to wait till 1928 before Rai Bahadur K.C. Sarkar arrives for precisely four months. Babu M.L. Dutta is even less enamoured in 1933, and gets his transfer in just three months. National integration begins with K.V.B. Pillai in 1936, but our man from Madras does no better than our men from Bengal, and is in office for just fourteen weeks. Khan Sahib G.Z. Abdin in 1937 can't take Chaibasa for more than ten days, while Rai Bahadur A.D. Banerjee in 1938 lasts out a full twenty before returning to the charms of Calcutta. N.P. Thandani goes six full months in 1938, but Rai Bahadur Rameshwar Singh restores the average by lasting only twenty-four days in 1939, and G.M. Ray creates some kind of a record by an official tenure of just four days in May 1944. K.N. Singh sees through independence and our first IAS officer turns up in 1952, B.P. Prasad. Mr Prasad stays four years.

Chaibasa, to put it mildly, was not a place where the Indian sahibs of the ICS cared to spend their youth.

The discussion in the background, as I stare at the roll of honour, deals with how to govern tribals. The secret, says one babu, is that one should not show one's face too often, otherwise these illiterate tribals begin to lose their awe of Government. One has to keep them properly afraid. '*Ghar Ki Murgi, dal barabar!*' he points out — the officer must be the occasional feast of chicken,- not the daily *dal*.

Later, the present DC, a fine example of the IAS, a little cynical about good intentions. but with reasonable commitment to liberalism and progress, describes the rationale of the Wilkinson Rules and the psyche of the tribal. 'When a child cries, and its mother does not hear, it will cry louder and louder on until its mother responds. The tribal will not cry. He will keep his resentment pent up until one day it bursts.'

One small story.

The dispute between the workers and the management of the mine began, ironically, over the distribution of sweets. But all that is unimportant. We will limit our story to what Deepak Varma, the District Superintendent of Police of Kiriburu, did to teach some 'errant' tribals a 'lesson.' He whipped them in public and then dragged them on the streets after tying them to the back of a police jeep.

All right, another story.

Ganga Ram Kalundia was given a medal for bravery by the President of India for his services in the army. Upon his retirement he involved himself in work among his people, and became a leader of the resistance to the dam over the river Kharkai which is part of the Rs.350 crore Subarnarekha Project. In the early hours of 4 April 1982 the police knocked on Kalundia's door; he tried to escape; the police fired, a bullet hit his leg; the police bundled him up and threw him into the van, destroyed and looted his house. On the way, near the village Soso, they bayoneted Kalundia to death in the van.

*

The first thing you see upon entering Chaibasa is a dramatic advertisement for *Jaan Ki Baazi*, showing at the Jain Movie Palace. (You would never suspect it, but the Jain family of Chaibasa is one of the biggest taxpayers in the country.) This is Tuesday, the day of the *hat* (market) and the city is alive with the din of commerce. Tribal women have brought sacks of rice, the men wood and woodcraft. This is their Sunday, and they are in their Sunday-best: the hair oiled and the one sari or *dhoti* in their possession freshly washed. Down the road from the market is the stadium of the Singbhum Sports Association. On the 21st, says an announcement, the semi-final match between the Damoria Block and the Khunitpani Block will take place; tickets 50 paise. Almost five years back, in March 1981, Narayan Jonko, Ashiwini Sammaiya and Christ Anand Topno held a public meeting at this stadium at which they demanded a separate country for the tribals, the State of Kolhanistan. Some of the promises made were fascinating; the proposed University of Kolhanistan, it was said, would be directly affiliated to Oxford (Topno and Jonko had just come back from a visit to England and Geneva where they had appealed for help from the UN and the Commonwealth Conference). Nobody took them very seriously to begin with, neither Delhi which had issued them with passports, nor Patna. There were a few scattered reports in the papers. But then suddenly one day the Government awoke. Topno and Sammaiya were arrested; Jonko was discovered to have gone underground.

The cry was an exaggeration of a child long denied a mother's attention, and it did not achieve more than passing impact. Jonko was the brain, and perhaps he was partly sponsored by those who would like to see a fragmented India. But the Topnos and Sammaiyas were manifestations of a long frustration, men fuelled by anger rather than mischief. Of course everyone dipped their hands into the current to see what flotsam would come their way. The mine-owners and the moneylenders who had robbed tribals turned every protest movement into a CIA den; the political parties turned it into electoral games. But there was a residual benefit too. Suddenly there was recognition that some glint of development had to be taken to this *bhumi*. A simple decision like the mobile Government shop can mean an enormous amount. Kerosene is sold by the mobile shop at Rs 2.30 per litre; the local shopkeeper charges Rs 5 or more in the interior. (Since there is no possibility of proper weights and measures, the soft drink bottle, with its measured capacity, comes in very handy.) The anger has provoked a trickle of change. And when you have not ever seen the miracle of clean water, the tubewell can be a wondrous sight.

One leg. A beautifully clean, cylindrical body, lean and straight. A neck which is a rod. On its head a metal walking stick, curved at the top and curved at the tail. This is the Goddess of Water. The tubewell. If gods and goddesses are symbols of need and fulfillment, fear and its containment, then perhaps the new deity of the tribals should be the tubewell. Wherever it has reached, its impact has been stunning. It is now the difference between the life styles of two villages. Kholkabad, the village at the foot of the hill on which is our bungalow, does not have a tubewell yet, but Gope, our guide, is confident that a sanction will come soon. That is his ambition before he retires as *chowkidar* of the bungalow in three years; to persuade the big sahibs who come to stay there to grant a tubewell to the village at their feet.

*

They make the stars differently in Saranda forest: in such thick and bright clusters that you feel that they might spill out of the sky at any moment. There is no moon that night as we walk down to the village, and the pool of shifting light formed by the torch seems an intrusion. We move towards the sound of the drum. A forest officer is with us, and doing all the talking. 'Want to see a dance,'he asks, hardly hiding the leer. Then adds regretfully, '*Hum log ka Ranchi main hiyan say jyada advanced naach hota hai.*' What he means is that the women in the tribal villages around Ranchi show more of their breasts than here. I ask him if he could organize the sleeping arrangements back in the bungalow; he goes back looking very busy and useful.

*

When the sun was rising
And the moon was large and beautiful in the sky
At such a wondrous moment were you born

There is great fun in their singing and dancing. The young people hold hands behind their backs, linking with one another in an affectionate, strong chain that goes back to the beginnings of their existence. Rice wine, warm and heavy and languorous, is being passed around. The presence of our guide, Gope, helps ease the tension which strangers bring to a family gathering. With some hesitation and then excitement we are offered the rice brew, the *handiya*. A lantern is placed beside me on a wood log. A woman comes and sits down a little beyond the lantern: the light falls on her face and on the faces of her her young children, the flame swaying slightly and forming patterns on the five faces: it is one of the most exquisite compositions I have ever seen. An old woman brings another leaf-cup of *handiya*, and teases, a little high herself, 'You should have come twenty years ago when I could have held you in my arms.' Gope translates and laughs. The banter is warm and wonderful; it is the ease of a confident culture that will always be outside the understanding of those who confuse 'advanced' learning with happiness.

> I did not see you in the village
> I did not see you in the market
> Should we go ahead and fall in love, stranger?

The young man with the flute joins us. He has been standing outside the line of young dancers. 'No, no, he could not join them,' he says: he is from another village, and if they ever hear that he has joined the dance here, it will be difficult for him to get married in his own village. We move away, and in the darkness meet a second group of young people. Just outside the line is Jugri, tipsy and jovial. 'Jugri is drunk,' Gope hears from his friend. Jugri sees us and shows off the transistor radio that he is holding and trying to tune (the batteries have clearly run out). 'This is a tape', he suddenly shouts. 'I am going to tape this song.' Everyone laughs. 'Look at Jugri; he says he is going to tape!' Jugri is teasing us — men from the world of the tape recorder. He shouts again: 'Disco!' He looks slyly at us amid the renewed laughter. Then he runs into the dancers and begins flirting outrageously with one of the girls. His wife is on the other side of the dancing line. She steps out, takes firm hold of Jugri and walks off. 'That is the end of Jugri's adventures for the night,' Gope laughs.

*

The beauty only adds to the pain: that there should be poverty in the core of so much that is so gloriously beautiful, the sky, the forest, the land, the laughter, the heart, the sharing, the openness. Everything becomes the victim of hunger and disease. The mother pointed proudly to her daughter, about six years old, and said, 'Today she had medicine!" Doctors from Tata Steel had come that day on one of their periodic missions and checked everyone; and that medicine was like a feast, a sudden opening of the heavens; it was not something that the mother could ever take as her right from a modern society. *'There is so real conflict between the human being and wildlife in their claims to the environment,'* one of the rusted boards had said at the gates of the forest, this time quoting Mrs Indira Gandhi. Yes, but the vicious conflict was surely between the co-aims of man and man. What was the difference between man and animal? That man could laugh? Or that man could be both poor and rich, while every animal was equally rich or equally poor. Or should the analogy be different? Was it a conceit to call animals by different names and treat man as a single species? Was it not more accurate to admit that there were the same differences in the human race too; that some were the vegetarian, huge brahminical elephants, jovial and learned, the *laddoo* in their palm, extremely equable when given their demanded place, and violent and roguish when angry; that some were lions among men, who had usurped, with their acquired might, the resources of the environment, who ate the flesh of others and proudly called themselves warriors and Singhs; that there were yet other men who were poisonous snakes, hissing their way through life, injecting the spittle of poison in communities, spreading lies and propaganda and their gospel of hate. And a caste of jackals, and then castes of the oppressed and the forgotten, denied by history and destiny their right to live as equals and as human beings, kicked, killed, smashed or simply spat upon, taunted and derided by the aggressors at the top...

Too much philosophy? Perhaps. But maybe one should be pardoned for a journey into thought when one reaches a forest where they make the stars differently.

February 1986

The Tomb of the Eunuch

Not a day has gone by in the Punjab without a few more innocent people falling victims to terrorist bullets. Hindus and Sikhs, who have lived together amicable for centuries, are now split apart. Batala, in 1985, was a symbol of the changing Punjab.

Patiala: The violence leapfrogs. Punjab has become an uneven chiaroscuro, the black and white shifting: the tragic paradox and sorrow of today's Punjab is that everything is normal and everyone is the next victim; Punjab is a lesson in how a few hundred terrorists, armed with modern weapons, can hold a people to ransom; blanket a society with that most dangerous of blinds, fear, so that ordinary and well-meaning people lose their composure and surrender their destinies temporarily to exploiters of one kind or another. The lumpen and the religous extremists know they cannot take over the State, they have neither the armed strength nor the popular support for that; but they know how to create the environment in which they can thrive. The real weapon of the terrorist is unpredictability; that is how he makes up for lack of numbers, through mobility and a completely amoral arbitrariness. Death jumps from Nakodar to Gurdaspur to Patiala to Batala to anywhere: there is no rationale in the choice of either place or victim (which is why as many Sikhs have died of terrorist gunfire as Hindus) except the creation of a fear psychosis. Each day's newspapers must carry a fresh crop of names from preferably yet another dot on the map.

And so Punjab provides the strange picture of normal life coexisting with sudden death; one part of a city bustling with cycles and buses and harried people continuing the difficult task of earning a living while silence rules the next street as curfew freezes all movement. The arteries of the State flow smoothly with traffic, the interruptions coming from the police searching for illegal arms or, perhaps, taking a look at your face to check whether it does not match some picture in a file. As we near Chandigarh a red light flashes in the darkness, becoming brighter as it nears: it is a police jeep patrolling the highway slowly, the light a luminous *tika* on its forehead. The policemen at the makeshift barrier on the highway, which has really become a permanent obstruction over these last three years, see the legend on the window of our car, 'Press,' and feel that the time has come for the first free gift of the day.

'*Koi Paper haegga*?' (Do you have any newspapers?) asks one, peering into our car in the hope that we are bringing the early editions from Delhi. I motion no. '*Ja Ja*,' he bellows in disgust: a non-existent bribe is clearly a poor way for a policeman to begin his day. A hoarding at this point on the road carries the message created for Jenson and Nicholson Paints: *Whenever you see colour think of us*, and the illustration is that of a watermelon in recognition of the coming hot season. The thought crosses one's mind that a drop of blood might have been more relevant as a symbol of the border of the Punjab. And yet, there is little sign of tension. Familiar cycles loaded with milk cans trundle by, and from across the fields comes the sound of pre-dawn prayers from a gurdwara. And, in the main city, there are early joggers scattered here and there, lonely advertisements for normalcy: after all, law and order is nothing more than feeling safe in the dark.

The feeling is reinforced along the way to Patiala: tractors and trucks bursting with the grain that has just begun to be harvested; squabbling public transport buses, rudely nosing one another out of the way; a liquor shop doing business at eight in the morning; a notice at the Guru Nanak Gas and Oil Company pointing out that petrol is cheaper here than in Chandigarh. Like so much of battle-scarred Punjab, the way is lined with monuments to fame and infamy. Soon we come upon the enormous gurdwara, Fatehgarh Saheb, in whose walls the sons of Guru Gobind Singh were buried by the Wazir of Sirhind We cross a Mughal bridge built by Jahangir (still functioning) and drive past a garden laid out by Akbar, the Amm Khaas Baagh. A massive and ugly harvester confronts us on the road: thanks to the troubles, there are fewer Biharis come in search of labour this year, and so the harvester is in expensive demand. The first indication that this is the Punjab of the newspaper headlines comes when we cross the railway lines and enter Patiala where on Monday one person died in a Sikh-Hindu communal riot and the administration ordered large parts of the town to go to sleep till sense returned.

The curfew in fact was restricted to the old city: but the shop-keepers of bazaars in the newer areas were not taking chances. Kashyap Sweets with its 'freezed soft drinks' had its shutters down, as had all its neighbours. Three policemen, enjoying their elevenses (glasses of milk) showed us the way to the District Commissioner's official residence. There was more activity along the Mall and in the market in front of the DC's house — a market clearly designed for the upwardly mobile Punjabi. Dewan Traders (the fun world of Leo toys) was open, but the establishments on either side were shut: Curly Tops (specialist in Latest Hair Style, Bridal Make-up, Facial, Bleach, Henna, Dyeing, Waxing and Perms) and Toe to Heels Shoes (gents). Video World, a little further down, was obviously going to be open for business on this enforced holiday, but GRD Travels (Passport Service, Air Tickets, Visa and Emigration Adviser) clearly considered it pointless to solicit potential departures on such a day. Aman's Galerie d' Garments (a boutique and subtitled in French!) and Temptations, the Chinese restaurant, were equally pessimistic.

An official car took us from the house to the DC's temporary office, in the former guest house for Englishmen built by the Maharaja of Patiala, and labelled, in the current crisis, the tactical headquarters. On the back seat of the car I saw my first naked revolver, a Smith and Wesson, and held it gingerly. The policemen driving and guarding me, sitting in front, nervously pointed out that it was loaded. I hastily abandoned my brief flirtation with ultimate power.

A stab in the back is a fairly normal human activity; but there are times when crime stops being an everyday statistic and turns into an act of war. On Monday, the evening of 7 April 1985, at about 7.30, an assistant in the PWD department got off the inter-city bus and went off for a drink. Gurbachan Singh had had a tiring day, having had to accompany his senior for a conference in the State capital, and could be forgiven for wanting a peg or two before returning home. No one is certain as to what transpired in that illegal bar with its mix of customers, but by 8.30 that night, the

35-year-old Government servant had been stabbed at Lahori Gate.

Word spread quickly, and groups of Sikh boys came out on the streets, brickbatting buildings and assaulting non-Sikhs. (The unfortunate Biharis who pull rickshaws always get the worst of these incidents; not only are they exposed, but their poverty and alienation makes them defenceless. 'You think twice before hitting a local *lala*,' one officer pointed out.) By 11.00 p.m., the DC, S.K. Sinha, had planned the deployment of forces, mapped out the lines of potential confrontation between the two communities (Khalsa mohalla, Jatta da Chautra, Arya Samaj chowk) and moved in the police to stop stray incidents. But the problem would really arise the next day, of course, when the extremists on both sides had had time to organize their arsenals and plans. The Senior Superintendent of Police (SSP) of Patiala, a very confident and even colourful officer, Gur Iqbal Singh, in the mean time had spread his men across the city. They had a common aim: for more than a year they had kept the peace in Patiala, never allowing any incident to spark off tension, and they were going to control matters now too. It would require the well-known tactical combination of the carrot and the stick, but they had both in plentiful supply and were not going to be miserly about the use of either.

Predictably the impetus for trouble came from the handful of All India Sikh Students Federation (AISSF) supporters, particularly the Manjit Singh group, who were gathered at the small gurdwara called the Naveen Singh Sabha. They were literally hysterical; one of them simply went for the Government officers with a brickbat during the discussions in which the officers were asking them not to take out any processions. They wanted the assailants caught by five that afternoon. They promised to do nothing till then but a hardcore dozen went ahead in any case to the Sher-e-Punjab market and other points, burnt two shops and brickbatted who they could. That was sufficient to trigger the response from the Hindu Suraksha Samiti and the All-India Hindu Students Federation (actually all these are rather grand names for more or less the same set of people). They retaliated by burning a Sikh shop. The pace of events sharpened with the funeral of the stabbed man; inevitably the 500-strong procession attacked Hindu establishments, and the latter fought back from their strongholds around the Kali Devi Mandir. By one that afternoon, the time for soft measures was over. Curfew was imposed.

Administration is a matter or nerve, sensibility and judiciousness. Precedent and the book have their great uses, but what do you do when faced by agent provocateurs armed with a deliberate plan to rend communities, stoke long-doused passion with mischief and lies so that a new and more devastating confrontation can make them more relevant, give them power and status in a society which would, by normal course, treat them as the scabs they are? The priest dreaming of his theocratic state or the lumpen searching for social legitimacy, the role of a protector during the breakdown of order, are not that far removed from each other: both need to destabilize and destroy existing social patterns through any means possible. Both have declared war on the State, and there is no morality in their conduct. The administrator, whose responsibility it is to protect the structures, must isolate the dangerous men who can inspire battle, discover those who have stings and then make them impotent.

One reason why Patiala was controlled quickly was because of the policing done before the trouble. Communalism became a factor in its life only after the refugees began to arrive after partition. The economic rivalry between the Sikh and Hindu trading classes only sharpened the animosity. The city became a traditional RSS base (Pawan Sharma, a communal Hindu leader, used to operate from here before Bluestar, the Army operation to rid the Golden Temple of Sikh militants). With the rise of Sant Bhindranwale's movement, the organization of the Sikh lumpen began. A typical 'extremist' in Patiala is Balbir Singh 'Sweety': in jail during Bluestar, released shortly after, School dropout, helper for a while in a truck which used to do the Punjab—Calcutta route, in his late teens, short, weak-looking, with no ostensible means of income. The Hindu youth leaders are financially better off, coming as they do from the trading classes, and blessed with some education but little learning. And in the middle are caught the ordinary people, sometimes, in sheer fright, the willing victims of such elements, but the rest of the time relieved to see them in another city, or in jail, or anywhere out of their lives.

And that is the great game that is going on in Punjab — the

effort for the control of the minds of the people. If the situation worsens, these divisive peddlers of fear will gain ascendancy. Each communal riot can only create one more leader of the AISSF or the Hindu Shiv Sena. And that is why the terrorists continue to kill, marking every day in the calendar with one more slash at the secular commitment which has kept these aspirant fascists in the obscurity which they deserve, rather than the power that they dream of. One defeat, in 1984 and 1985, was not enough for them. They are giving battle again: and perhaps it was naive to imagine that they would surrender after the end of only the first war. The second war for Khalistan is currently underway, and the battles are being fought on myriad fronts.

*

Barely ten kilometres from Batala is the gurdwara Gurudarshan Prakash, its dome gleaming: here, at Chowk Mehta, is the head-quarters of the Damdami Taksal, the order which Sant Jarnail Singh Bhindranwale lifted from obscurity into a household term, with a power that now competes with the Shiromani Gurdwara Parbandhak Committee (SGPC). It is quiet this morning, with the faithful going about their usual tasks, the priests dressed in the style — the robe ending a little below the knees and the turban knotted in a distinctive, flat manner — which Bhindranwale made famous. The youthful priest we talk to is not in the least embarrassed to discuss the ambition of Khalistan which, of course, is to him the real hallmark of a true Sikh. All arguments are met with a smile and an answer which may or may not have either truth or logic. It is true, isn't it, that the pro-Khalistanis were badly defeated in the free elections? 'Ah, but do you know of any honest man who has won in these things called elections? Selection, not election, is the way to find leaders.'

The Barnala Government was made by the people... 'The Akalis are stooges of Rajiv Gandhi,' he says, and then adds, 'Our religion cannot be divorced from politics. Only those who protect our religion can be entrusted with our politics.' But over and over again the Akalis have shown they have the support of the Sikh people — witness their *Sarbat Khalsa* (General Assembly) at Anandpur Sahib.

'That was only full of Government employees. Our *Sarbat Khalsa* on 13 April will be the real one.' And if no one turns up? 'The Government is doing everything possible to stop our supporters from coming.' A little later the conversation turns to whom he regards as the successor to Bhindranwale. 'Bhai Mokham Singh,' he says simply.

Police Chief Julius Ribeiro issued a statement just this week that on no condition would Bhai Mokham Singh, who is under detention, be released. The memories of the flip-flop over the detention of Sant Bhindranwale still rankles.

And could our friend, the priest, tell us anything about the sieges of Batala, when Sikhs from the villages, in unconscious repetition of Mao Zedong's dictum, besieged the city? A smile. 'Nothing. I know nothing at all.' But surely... 'You will have to ask the villagers themselves.'

Batala goes back a long while in history; it is as old, if not older, than Amritsar. A little before the modern town, and facing the large bungalows that are still springing up as the wealthy continue to grow richer, is the famous shrine of Shamsher Khan, known and loved in Batala as the Baba. A notice board put up by the Archaeological Department, which took up the protection of this monument less than two decades ago, provides a taut outline: 'Shamsher Khan, a eunuch and *karori* of Batala, was buried in this monument in Akbar's time. He was a *Faujdar* (soldier) of Manikpur.' (It is only in the 'liberated' modern world that the genetic sexual deficiency that makes a eunuch is sufficient to condemn such a person to a life of degradation. There was no such prejudice earlier, and eunuchs made some notable warriors and administrators.)

Before Partition, Batala was a Muslim majority town; today, of course, the Muslims are all gone, uprooted by Partition and replaced by those old mosques now inhabited by refugees. But though half of Batala is Hindu and the other half Sikh, every Friday lamps are still lit at the *mazaar* (shrine) and the people come to pray at the tomb of their Baba, unconscious that religion could be any dividing line. They believe that their Baba will intercede on their behalf with God and ensure a harvest, or bring a child to a hopeful mother, or help a son pass an examination or get a job, or do one or the other of a hundred things by which we define

happiness in this world. And every Friday night, someone or the
other sees an apparition of the Baba, in a white tunic and a green
tahmat, riding a horse, and they all say that he looks more hand-
some than a bridegroom. Kalu Ram has personally seen the Baba,
and he insists that the Baba comes especially in time of trouble.
Kalu Ram was appointed by the Archaeological Department in
1972 as attendant, and each day he sweeps the octagonal shrine,
the tomb at the centre of the octagon, the eight arches forming the
walls over which a large and typically beautiful Mughal dome
rises, engraved inside with verses from the Quran. A staircase
winds up to a circular passage upstairs, and although it looks
simple you can get lost: it is called the Bhul Bhawan. When the
troubles of 1984 took place, Kalu Ram got afraid and took shelter
in this Bhawan along with his family. His wife clearly saw the Baba
sitting on a charpoy outside, wearing Kalu's uniform as a signal of
his concern. The stories are endless: and no one doubts them even a
little.

The Baba, as his designation implies, was once a great cavalry
man, but one day he heard a voice telling him to give up killing,
and from that day he became a fakir. He built his mausoleum
himself. Over his grave, on a metal chain, was a golden gong,
which used to be beaten to announce the time of worship. Once, no
one quite remembers when, some thieves came to steal the gong.
No sooner had they taken it and gone outside than their throats
were cut mysteriously. The outside of each of the seven arches (the
eighth makes the doorway) is, believe it or not, splashed with what
looks undoubtedly like blood stains, as if blood had spurted there
and then trickled down. The amazing thing is that it cannot be
washed or wiped off; there is some chemistry that keeps the stains
fresh through rain and heat. Kalu Ram has seen them for fourteen
years, and generations before him have done so too. There is a
tunnel below, guarded by snakes. And discoveries are still being
made. Just three years or so ago, a possessed woman came and told
the attendant to dig under a *ganja* plant growing wild in the
courtyard: a well was discovered, just as she had predicted,
hundreds of years after being forgotten.

Punjab, for centuries on the crossroads of armies and ideas and
religions and cultures, a scene of bitter conflict and unique resolution, land of Hindu, Muslim and Sikh, maintained its social

harmony because of this great tradition of holy men who spread a message of peace and equality and were held in the highest reverence by all. In the face of feudal violence, and often persecution, they made their own lives examples of the ideals they preached. Since the Muslim Babas were buried, their graves became shrines at which everyone bowed their heads; the Hindus and Sikhs were remembered through song and story and proverb and dictum. But, of course, they could not eradicate the violence of men. There were always times in history when the world turned to the wars they had warned against.

*

They used to call him, *Chuha*, or the Mouse, in derision. Now he is a leader. And Soma was a pickpocket; now he travels on a scooter, has money in his pocket, and women flock to the Government office to demand his release if he is placed under custody. They are the heroes in today's Batala.

Once again, the outsider would be astonished upon entering this town only recently besieged by about 20,000 or more Sikhs, and still under partial curfew, at the sight of Hindus and Sikhs intermingling publicly as if the newspaper reports were all fraudulent. In quick succession my guide, a young and extremely sensible man called Kanwarjeet, a leader in his class in the Baring Union Christian College, was greeted by a Shiv Sena youth, Naresh Chanda, and an AISSF teenager, Harendar Singh. How had he achieved this status? I asked, teasing a little. He paused before answering seriously, 'I am neither a Sikh nor a Hindu. I am a Thakur.' Obviously the few Thakurs there saw themselves above a fray engineered, in their opinion, largely by Bhapas and *Lalas*.

The first communal clash between Sikhs and Hindus that he could remember was in March 1984; brickbats were thrown on a Hindu procession by boys from the Nanak College. The second took place by the end of the year: There was arson and a police lathi charge. In the third clash, the arson had doubled and bullets killed one person. In the fourth, the latest, bombs and bullets were the main weapons.

He was sure why the riots had been engineered. At the heart of it was economic gain, and as the tension built around the tussle, more and more manipulators dipped their hands in to exploit the situation and make their share of cash. He gave evidence which would be libellous to print, but would sound valid to anyone who has seen communal riots from close quarters. These after all are the wars of black money.

The origins of this latest outburst of violence were simple to the point of being idiotic. Formally, it all began over a rickshaw ride.

It is only a short distance between the Nehru Gate and the Sat Kartari gurdwara: and the road is crowded in typically North Indian fashion with traffic and shoppers. In front of the gurdwara is the Indra (sic) Gandhi Clinic (donated by the Factories' Association, Batala). Behind the Nehru Gate is the Chakri Bazaar, with its narrow lanes packed on either side by shops; this is the Hindu stronghold. Behind the gurdwara is the Sikh bastion: not surprisingly, any fighting that has to be done goes on in the intervening space. And here the rickshaw in which the Sikh was traveling hit a scooter. Interestingly, both the rickshaw puller and the scooter driver were Hindus, and the Sikh was, at least according to his sympathizers, only trying to pacify both. But by the time the quarrel had developed, everyone, including a few people from the vegetable bazaar adjoining the gurdwara, had joined in and turned against the Sikh, who eventually managed to run into the gurdwara and take sanctuary. A little later brickbats and bullets were whizzing between the two sides.

A stupid incident had destroyed a fragile peace. The problem really started over the land surrounding the gurdwara, which contains the vegetable market. The original shopkeepers who rented it are paying old rents — about Rs. 20 or so per shop. And they have sublet every square foot in their shops to other vegetable sellers, in return for as much as Rs.20-25 a day. The gurdwara, which owns the shops, is naturally irritated and has been asking for the land to be returned to build a pool. The Hindus are in no mood to do so.

After the violence broke out in Batala, some Sikhs rushed out to the villages with stories of women being raped and the gurdwara being destroyed. These baseless allegations inflamed passions and before the administration realized what was happening, about 20,000 armed Sikhs had surrounded Batala. What could have been a horrifying conclusion was calmed when the administration finally managed to show the representatives of the Sikhs outside the city that nothing had in fact happened to the gurdwara.

The point, of course, is that Batala will build and burst again, as each pause in the battle gives time to the manipulators to plan the next twist of the screw. The new protectors of the Hindus, resplendent in their fresh status, have now developed as great a vested interest in confrontation as the extremists. Gradually the number of cities being drawn into the widening net of communalism is increasing — Jalandhar to Ludhiana to Batala to Patiala to...

There are no Babas today who have heard a voice in the night telling them to give up killing and spread the message of peace. The achievement of Mahatma Gandhi is dismissed cynically as somehow outdated, perhaps even a fluke possible only in extraordinary circumstances by an extraordinary individual. The modern fashion is the politics of cynicism. Granted, cynicism might prove a temporary bandage, but to confuse it with medicine is dangerous delusion.

If Punjab is going to be healed it will have to be done by those who wear no disguise, who have never worn them, not by communalists masquerading under one spurious ideology or the other. The firmness with criminals must be evenhanded, just as the resolve to restore peace without manipulation and without arrogance must be firm, an outcome of genuine conviction and courage. There is evil abroad, and it seems we are just too embarrassed to recognize the one weapon which has been successful against it in our history: the philosophy of decency, of goodness, of strength in brotherhood and faith in interdependence.

February 1986

God's Martyrs

The dispute over the Ram Janma Bhumi temple/Babari Masjid in Ayodhya has given both Hindu and Muslim hate-mongers enough excuse to exploit their respective communities. Fortunately there are some sane elements in this dangerously volatile situation —as in the village called Bhanauli where Hindus refused to allow Hindu mobs or the police to do violence to their Muslim fellow-villagers. A report from the historic city of Ayodhya where the temple/mosque is situated.

Ayodhya: More men have died in the defence of belief than truth: men will gladly offer their blood, become heroes and martyrs spurred by conviction, conquer nations in the name of superiority, and raise murder to a virtue in the defence of a piece of cloth. Those in power know this, and perhaps this is why they are in power. And of all the ideas that have either inspired men to achievement or driven them to suicide, none has been more glorious or more dangerous than the concept of God. It is perhaps our ultimate conceit that we need to defend our version of Him, or that He cannot survive the decay of an institution in His name.

Temples and mosques are stones held together by design; a design of geometry, true, but foremost, a design of the mind. If they were only symbols of God, which is what they were meant to be, then there would be little problem. It is when they become extensions of the vanity, predijuces and ambitions of men, when they become showpieces of human power, that they become battle-fields. Once, that acre of land on which lies the three-domed Babari Masjid of the Muslims and the birthplace of Ram for the Hindus, was shared. Both would come and offer their different forms of worship, the Muslims bowing to Allah in the courtyard of the mosque, the Hindus worshiping at the *chabutara* (platform) just outside on the left of the gate. In time everything changed. Mahant Raghubar Das filed a suit with the Sub-judge at Faizabad (the district headquarters) for permission to build a temple on the *chabutara* to commemorate the birthplace of Bhagwan Ram Chandra; he had come to court because the Deputy Commissioner of Faizabad had prohibited the construction of the temple after objections raised by Muslims. Tensions rose, and one day the inevitable flashpoint was reached. Muslims *shaheeds* (martyrs) gathered in their fortified Babari Masjid and their Hindu equivalents massed at the nearby Hanuman Garhi, barely a hundred yards away. The two sides, charged and counter-charged, at one point the Muslims nearly taking Hanuman Garhi. The Hindus were more successful eventually and at the end of the day they had captured the Babari Masjid, leaving seventy-five Muslims dead (the graveyard of Ganjshaheed marks the battle). The police were present but merely looked on, being under strict orders not to interfere.

This happened exactly one hundred years ago, in 1885.

The judge took that martial victory away. His rationale was simple: 'Awarding permission to construct the temple at this juncture is to lay the foundation of riot and murder.' The name of the judge was Pandit Hari Kishan.

The Englishman who reported this incident for the Government's records did not hide the truth of an amicable past. A.F. Millett, the officiating settlement officer mentions, 'It is said that upto that time (the riot of 1885) the Hindus and Mohammedans alike used to worship in the mosque/temple. Since British rule a railing has been put up to prevent disputes, within which, in the mosque, the Mohammedans pray, while outside the fence the Hindus have raised a platform on which they make their offerings.' And then in the last quarter of the nineteenth century, the first propagators of modern communalism, the builders of a nation in the name of religion, first came into prominence. These ideologues sent out their missionaries — priests, politicians, novelists, historians — to colour the mind of an emerging nation with blood rather than peace. The growing synthesis among the upper and middle classes and the creation of a common culture among the poor was the target. 'Purification' became the key of separation, as the leaders indulged in dreams of Muslim and Hindu states. The effort began to destroy symbols and poison occasions common to both Muslims and Hindus — for instance, the *tazia* procession at Moharrum (Hindu women believed that they would get a child if they walked under the *tazia*) and the shared happiness at Diwali. The communalization of life began with the intellectuals, and the message was thrust down. But it was difficult, because the people resisted. The ideologies could turn Hinduism into Sanskritization and Islam into Arabization but the people still believed in Hindustani or their traditional spoken languages, and respect for the fakir or the *mahatma*. The communalists had only one really good weapon: fear. Fear was the bow, and a whisper was the arrow. They told the Muslims that the Hindus would destroy their mosques, the laws, their way of life, by the sheer weight of numbers and the help of a partial administration. They told the Hindus that Muslims were foreigners who would always kill and oppress, whose loyalty to this land would ever be doubtful. And every potential point of friction was seized and sharpened. The surprise is not that they found such points of dispute, but that, in a subcontinent as large as ours, with a history as tortured as ours (and historians as pernicious as ours), they could not find more. But a mosque allegedly built on the birthplace of Bhagwan Ram Chandra (Lord Rama) was quite tailormade for tension.

There is great subtlety in this. If there is any symbol of the rule of perfect justice and tolerance it is *Ram Rajya*; when Gandhiji dreamt of a *Ram Rajya* he was promising the minorities and the untouchables a state of equality and freedom. And Babar was one Muslim emperor whose broad tolerance has not been challenged by even the fanatic historians. If Hindus can be convinced that even Ram cannot get the respect of Muslims, then their sentiment can be much more easily roused. And if even Babar cannot be considered acceptable, then the Muslim, in turn, feels desperate — what more must he do to become acceptable. Become a Hindu?

*

A hundred years after 1885, so many civil wars and partitions later, the game of blood and revenge is still being played. But if the India of the communalist has not died as yet, neither has the India of harmony. If I was depressed by the first on the road to Ayodhya, I was also elated by the second — visible to those who want to see it, and on the same road.

The shrine industry is already there in full strength; sweetmeat-flower-and beads-shops line the street rising at a slight gradient towards the high ground atop which sits the disputed mosque. Monkeys prance about, but that is understandable; one of them tweaks the tail of a yelping pup and will not release it until the owner turns up. Equally understandable is the sale of literature published by various Hindu organizations 'authenticating' the birthplace of Ram. 'Nine hundred thousand years ago,' begins the pamphlet titled *The Romantic History of Sri Ram Janmabhumi*, 'on this holy spot the great god Sri Ram Chandraji manifested himself...' And then come details of how Raja Vikramaditya built on this spot one of the four great temples of the old world, before the coward Babar, licking his wounds after being defeated by Raja Sangram Singh, destroyed.. and so on and so forth. Other pamphlets are neither more convincing or less venomous against Muslims. On the *chabutara outside the premises, priests are singing bhajans*: the *kirtan* has not stopped since 27 December 1949 when another court order put a lock on the main building. Photography is prohibited, says a Government notice, and perhaps that is a sensible decision, since photographs could be inflammatory. Another Government notice board in front of the iron railings put up by the British explains that this ancient monument is *wiwad grast*, a term much more evocative than the its dry English translation, disputed. The stream of pilgrims —simple village folk, coming in hundreds each day — is constant and the sale of garlands brisk. Popular verses are painted on the walls of the small enclosure beyond the door where the idols and pictures of Ram and Hanuman have been placed. The rest of the area is sealed off; that is, of course, the courtyard of the mosque. I try and enter and am firmly prevented by the PAC guard: he did not let even the city magistrate pass the previous day, who am I to try and do so? The formal evidence offered to prove that there indeed was an older temple commemorating the birthplace of Ram is two carved, short, black pillars holding up the arch that forms the large doorway; it is believed that these were among the eighty-four such pillars, brought back by Ram and Hanuman after their victory in Lanka. Others provide different kinds of corroboration. In a signed pamphlet being distributed, a former Congress minister of Uttar Pradesh, Dua Dayal Khanna, says that Aurangzeb has admitted in his *Alimgirnama* that on the seventh of Ramzan 1684, he had to seize the temple and destroy it again after it had been restored to Hindu hands by Sikhs and Hindus under Guru Gobind Singh. There is a small problem here; if the *Alimgirnama* does mention the figure 1684, then we will have to wait another 200 years for the day to come since all the dates were in Hijri (the Muslim Calender) then. And if Mr Khanna has converted the date, then it is still a surprise since Aurangzeb was in the Deccan from 1682 to 1707. But all this argument is a bit irrelevant as is the highly laboured 'reply' given by Muslim leaders. The point is that the common Hindus believe that this really is the birthplace of Ram, and arrive each day, with simplicity and devotion, to pay homage to a God who is part of their psyche. And it is equally certain that the common Muslim feels that a mosque in which he has prayed for generations is being robbed of him. It is not truth which is at issue, but belief. Evidence can take us to a rational approximation of the truth, but how does one deal with belief? Which Solomon can divide this child? What is the truth? asks one pamphlet published by the Tahaffuz-i-Masjid Committee situated at Gwynne Road, Lucknow. The truth is larger than what is accepted in their pamphlet — that through the Twenties and Thirties, when the mosque was under the control of Muslims, it was mismanaged and neglected and that the district Waqf Commissioner of Faizabad was forced to condemn the *muttwalii* as an opium addict in a report signed 16 September 1938, that few Muslims seemed so devout as to care about even such an obviously high-profile place until it became a target, that its keepers were more interested in the *waqf* income than in devotion. And that, no matter what their claims might be, there has always been this dispute over the spot, and that the British often referred to it in their files as the Janmasthan Mosque of Ajoodhia — an appellation which did not seem to bother the *muttwalii* when he referred to the British for arbitration on *waqf* claims?

But the problem, as said before, it not the truth, but the whisper. That whisper is travelling through the towns and villages of the north of India, becoming a swirl, kicking up puffs of hate, and if it is not calmed, it will become a storm. And the Government of

Uttar Pradesh, for two weeks after the place was opened by a court order, looked piously the other way when the mischief was being done. In fact, it gave the whisper a microphone. And only when the sound echoed in the Parliamentary constituency of Amethi, represented in the Lok Sabha by Rajiv Gandhi, did it seem to look back — in feigned surprise.

For months now, the men who have made their beards synonymous with the Muslim destiny in our country, have been spreading their whisper: Islam is in danger! Their provocation was yet another judgement: the Supreme Court decision to grant an old lady called Shah Bano a higher maintenance, after her divorce, than her husband was prepared to offer. Perhaps this particular storm might have remained in the teacup were it not for a few unnecessary remarks accompanying the judgement. But the chance came and it was seized. A national movement developed among the Muslims demanding that the Muslim Personal Law* be placed beyond the purview of the courts. As the nerve of insecurity was touched, the Muslims responded; and even women, who could only benefit from the judgement, were persuaded to rally to the cause. Public meetings, demonstrations, protests, flags, marches created headlines. The persistence with which known Hindu communalists began to demand progress among the Muslims only strengthened the minority conservatives, whose credibility could only go up with each statement from the RSS. In this tinder box came the order of the District and Sessions Judge of Faizabad, K.M.Pandey, to open the locks of the disputed mosque/temple and implicitly allow the priests to enter which they did.

The UP Government says it knew nothing about this order and the administrative aftermath, which takes some believing. In any case, there is no excuse for what followed. In city after city, victory processions were taken out celebrating the 'liberation' of the Ram Janmabhumi Temple, and everywhere slogans designed to provoke Muslims rent the air. The terrifying part was not that the tension was rising in cities like Aligarh, where the tension in any case hardly ever comes down, but that it was seeping into villages which had not seen riots since Partition. One is deliberately not

---

*is based on the Quran: while civil law is the same for everyone, Muslims conduct their personal affairs like marriage according to the precepts of Islam.

reporting the slogans: adding currency to them will not help. But they were shouted over microphones by voice and through cassette, and soon town after town became a medley of black and saffron flags as the divided communities became increasingly hostile. Something had to give. It did. Among other places, at Musafirkhana.

Curfew is a trifle meaningless in a village, for the simple reason that no one understands it; and it has not much more than psychological value in the one-street town, apart from limiting traffic along the particular highway. Ayodhya and Faizabad were free, but the whole stretch of highway between adjoining Sultanpur and Musafirkhana was under curfew by Wednesday. Death had come the previous Monday.

All through the day before, the loudspeakers had blared their message of victory laced with taunts from the bazaar of Musafirkhana. By nine the next morning, the *rath yatra* (chariot procession) travelling through the area reached Musafirkhana. And the attack on Muslim shops and houses along the street began. The police stood and watched when they were not directly encouraging the rioters. The gutted houses and shops are going to remain in evidence long after the curfew is lifted. But the number was limited for the simple reason that there were no more shops or houses to burn and loot. The real target of the rioters was a village called Bhanauli, just a little off the road, across the railway line, hardly five minutes away from Musafirkhana. This large village has, like so many others in central and western Uttar Pradesh, a fifty per cent Muslim population. And it was here that the values that still preserve the heart of this subcontinent prevailed.

Many of the Muslims living in Musafirkhana had taken shelter in Bhanauli, and the mob, having completed its looting in the town, was being urged by its leaders towards the village. At this point, the most prominent Hindus of Bhanauli including Ram Bali, Sheo Narayan, Ram Khilawan and Guddu came out of their homes and stood outside the village. Others joined them, including most touchingly, children, and they told the rioters that they would not allow a single Muslim in their village to be hurt. They had grown up together and they were friends; an attack on the Muslims was an attack on them. The police — of the Provincial Armed Constabulary — were with the mob and actually began encouraging the mob not to listen to these sentimentalis. Kalahu, whose house is on the edge, says that he was repeatedly urged by a policeman to start the violence and looting but refused. All the Muslims of Bhanauli concur with every word of this. It there are any awards for integrity in our country, Bhanauli deserves them all. As for the police, nothing much will happen to them as usual. The officer in charge of the police station of Musafirkhana has been suspended, but it will be too much to expect the Government to do anything more than quietly reinstate him when the heat has abated.

*

The graveyard is serene and ancient . The tombstones are black and jagged with neglect, and the curved closed arches of the grave chipped and peeling with age: the last monuments of generations of minor nobility (mud is good enough for the poor). The cemetery of Ayodhya is at the edge of the town, on the other side from the river Saryu on whose banks lie the medley of temples. Finding it is not difficult, but we have to ask often for directions to my destination, the tomb of Shea, believed to be the grandson of Adam by the Muslims. Prahlad Yadav finally directs us towards the spot. He is wearing a locket with a picture on it .

'Who is that?' I ask.'Thakur Onkar Nath,' he replies, 'A great *mahatma* of Calcutta'.

We are following an unusual story we have heard in Lucknow: that the Muslims of Ayodhya believe that the grandson of Adam is buried in their city. Prahlad Yadav knows about that *mazaar*. Does he believe in both his *mahatma* and the *mazaar*? I ask. He smiles shyly and says '*Ek hi baat hai*' (it is all the same).'

There is something surely in the land of Ayodhya which connects it to man's earliest perceived spirituality — for the Hindus, Ram ; for the Muslims, the grandson of Adam. The grave is simple, a little larger than usual, painted a thin white in deference, and situated in the shade of spreading tamarind and bel trees. A door guards the entrance, but there is no roof. Gangaprasad Upadhyay, a lecturer in the local intermediate college, is going home on his bicycle along the dusty track when we stop him. 'Yes, this is a holy site for the Muslims; no one's prayer is ever turned down.' And once a year, he says, the spirits of all the fakirs are said to gather at this *mazaar*.

On the other side of the city, progress has shifted the bank of the river away from the old waterfront as land has been created to construct a new bridge across the Saryu. But life in the temples and the *dharamshalas* (rest-houses for pilgrims) goes on in much the same way as it has for centuries: a teenaged Brahimn boy, his head freshly shaved, the tuft hanging from his head, oils his body in the morning sun; sadhus sit chatting with each other; the sound of the occasional prayer wafts across as you walk down; at a water tap, two men are washing their clothes. In the teashops men are chatting easily. A slogan appears on the wall: *Sudhir Pande mast hai, sabki zamanat zapt hai* (Sudhir Pande is our man, the others will lose their deposits).

In a pleasantly startling sight, you see a fully painted sadhu cycling confidently towards his destination. Small shops sell their myriad wares. Trinkets fill the stalls meant for the pilgrims: glass birds, toy boats powered by wick flames chugging over the water in a large bowl, bangles, the Veena Fine View Scope Binocular, pictures of Ram and Hanuman hugging each other, plastic trains on plastic tracks, cars made by Sanjay Plastic Industries, whirlers, tin birds, hair clips, drums, rings, cardboard cutouts, embedded with glass, of elephants and butterflies... Ayodhya seems at remarkable peace with itself for a city which has lit fires across the country. Hindus and Muslims, waiting for each other in city after city, from Calcutta to Jammu, who till a fortnight ago did not know that such a temple or a mosque even existed but did know that they had wounds to reopen, have come out on to the streets, sometimes with the torch in their hand, sometimes the knife, and always the roar that echoes and frightens, that makes a child quiet with dread and a mother tremble, in the defence of their pieces of cloth —the saffron of the *bhagwa* or the green with the moon. The grip of fear transcends quickly to hate, and hate erupts into a stab. And the fear spreads. Today and this week will once again test the humanity of human beings.

February 1986

Gorkhaland's Historical Imperative

The Gorkhas' demand for a separate State of their own. Gorkha-
land, lies rooted in a controversial past. Schemes of autonomy for
the Gorkha region have been on the anvil for several decades now.
And, ironically, these schemes later got the vociferous support of
the Communist Party of India.

The saddest element of this story is that the Gorkhas are such a
lovely people; watching their familiar smiles explode into anger
seems like an expression of some deep failure. They are a simple,
even innocent, people and perhaps they have become victims of
their own innocence. But then nothing is ever quite what it seems in
our country, particularly when the artists of manipulation like
Subhas Ghising are at work, sewing truth with conjecture, distortion and outright lie to create patterns that frighten and inflame
human beings; and of course no weapon is more valuable than a
selective past. The people become puppets, dancing on the strands
of a complex web, entertaining only the manipulators and wound-
ing only themselves.

Like all our experiences about unity and separation, we must go
back deep into our colonial past.

There is nothing new about the Gorkha demand for separation
from 'Bengali-dominated' Calcutta. When the great protectors of
the British empire, the Lords Morley and Minto, were in the
process of formally communalizing Indian politics with their
'reforms' in which lay the idea of separate electorates, they enter-
tained a demand from the hill people for a separate administrative
set-up for the district of Darjeeling. This was in 1907, exactly one
year after the first delegation of the Muslim League got an audience
with the Viceroy. By 1917, when the next set of reforms were being
offered, the hillmen had expanded their ambition: they wanted 'the

creation of a separate unit comprising the present Darjeeling district with the portion of Jalpaiguri district which was annexed from Bhutan in 1865.' And they left open the possibility of a larger area including parts east of Bhutan and the Assam Dooars.

When the Simon Commission came in 1928, the same plea was given another hearing. And then, before the passage of the critical Government of India Act of 1935, Sir Samuel Hoare, then Secretary of State for India, received a delegation led by Sardar Bahadur S.W. Laden La (the main road to Darjeeling is named after him) on 6 August 1934. The demand: 'The district of Darjeeling should be totally excluded from Bengal and an independent administrative unit created with an administration at the head of the area, assisted by the executive council.'

By 1943 the All India Gorkha League had come into existence. In a petition to Jawaharlal Nehru on 20 April 1952, it described its position as 'a more statesmanlike view' and demanded that ' the district of Darjeeling together with the Dooars section of Jalpaiguri be included in the province of Assam.' This plea was also made before the Cabinet Mission.

The British, generally quite generous about partitioning other people's lands, were hesitant about this particular demand, presumably because they were worried about the implications of a consolidation of Gorkha interests and power in a specific land area on the border of Nepal. At the one time when they took Darjeeling out of Bengal, between 1907 and 1912, they did not give it autonomy, but tagged it on to the Bhagalpur division. The reason? *Lipi* (Script). The common use of Devnagari by the Nepalese and the Hindi-speaking people made administration simpler, at least in theory. But when Bengal was reunited, Darjeeling came back. However, the British did keep the district a non regulated area: in other words, laws passed by the Bengal Council were not applicable in the region unless specified. In 1935, Darjeeling was made Partially Excluded as before. These distinctions disappeared with freedom in 1947. But the Government of Dr P.C. Ghosh was careful to keep some of the distinctions (which worked against Nepalis) in force as, for instance, the practice of nominating members to district boards and municipalities. All over Bengal this was abolished, except in Darjeeling. The Ghosh Government wanted to retain the power to nominate Bengalis onto the boards in Darjeeling, fearing that no Bengali might survive an adult franchise election.

Though the British did not accept the demand, they always encouraged it by the simple ruse of constantly entertaining it. But this was understandable, since it conformed to a policy practiced by them all over the country. But if the separatist demand has taken an ugly turn almost forty years after the British left, it is not because Sardar Bahadur Laden La was given an audience with the White Sahib. It is because in one way or another Indian political parties have continuously wooed the Gorkhas with the promise of autonomy. The most important of these were the Communists, not only because their Darjeeling unit was inspired and headed by a Gorkha who led the call for autonomy, but also because the Communists (in the incarnation of the CPI (M) came to power in the State. The constant reiteration of the demand for autonomy kept the hope alive in the Gorkha consciousness, even if its equally determined rejection each time by the Centre fuelled the Gorkha frustration. The Communist Party of India used the demand for Gorkha autonomy in the forties and the Fifties to create a base in the hill areas, and then expanded and detailed this promise when it was making its most ambitious bid for power, in 1970, at the time when the United Front in Bengal was dying and the next stable Government was not yet visible on the horizon.

After all, what was the perception of the Communist support for autonomy among the Gorkhas? Simply this: that a party full of Bengalis spread all across the State had accepted the Gorkha contention that the Gorkha language, identity and economic development would never be possible as long as their district was ruled by Bengalis.

*

Rattanlal Brahmin is old now, and his voice has become feeble, both literally and in party circles, but his views have not changed since the Forties: he tells anyone who will listen that the Gorkha must have his autonomy. In the Forties the voice of Brahmin echoed in the hills. He was instrumental, with some help from plains' leaders like Charu Mazumdar and Sourin Bose, in forming the district unit of the undivided Communist Party of India and his strategy for spreading Communist influence was simple exploitation of the latent disaffection of the Gorkhas against Bengalis. In fact, among the very first things he did, in the mid-Forties, was to organize a resolution by the Darjeeling unit of the party for regional autonomy to the hill region. The CPI endorsed the proposal. One worker who was party to the proposal was Ananda Mohan Pathak, now a Member of Parliament. So effective was this that Rattanlal Brahmin won a seat in the Bengal Council in the elections of 1946. In Calcutta, the leader, Jyoti Basu, raised the cry when Dr B.C. Roy was Chief Minister, demanding 'regional autonomy for the Gorkhas within the State of West Bengal.' Mr Basu was careful in his stresses, but the Darjeeling unit of the CPI was not. In any case, the constant harping on the theme that the 'economic and cultural development' of the Gorkhas was impossible without autonomy gave implicit legitimacy to the idea that the Gorkhas would never be treated as equals by the Bengalis, and that survival in Bengal was synonymous with oppression. Inevitably, in the early Fifties, a booklet in Nepali began doing the rounds demanding 'Gorkhasthan.' While the CPI never formally supported any such move, its local unit was definitely involved.

In fact, the Communists, in their eagerness to nurture their support base in the hills, went even further ahead than the Gorkha League in their chant for a 'sthan.' Deo Prokash Rai, the legendary Gorkha leader, and then the secretary of the Darjeeling unit of the League, was compelled to write to the press to distance his party from the Communists and from such a 'Gorkhasthan.' Rai wrote that he deemed it his 'bounden duty' to clarify that the Gorkha League could not be clubbed with the Communists. 'The mention of the Communist Party together with the name of my organization.. cannot but be taken strong exception to... The people are already waiting for the bugle call not for the creation of any "Sthan" but for the onward march in the struggle for survival as equal human beings.' While ending the letter Rai made specific reference to the theocrats who had demanded 'sthans' so recently, and clearly differentiated the League from such elements: 'I would venture to say that the true feelings of the masses do not repose in the hearts of any pundit, padre or rabbi, but they lie with those men, those communities whose names are never seen in the headlines of newspapers, nor heard of from the lips of any pundit, padre of rabbi.'

The formal position of the Gorkha League was set out in the memorandum to Jawaharlal Nehru submitted on 29 April 1952 by N.B. Gurung, then President of the League: separation, since 'two generations of the hill people have in clear terms expressed their will to break away from Bengal.' The League than indicated that it was willing to accept any of the three options which were being mooted: (i) that the district be a separate administrative unit directly administered by the Centre; (ii) that a separate province be set up comprising the district of Darjeeling and the neighbouring areas, (iii) that the district of Darjeeling with a section of Jalpaiguri viz the Dooars be included in Assam.'

The split in the Communist movement did not affect this policy; the CPI (M) continued to identify itself with autonomy. A formal statement by the party indicates what it was prepared to concede, and a few quotes will confirm how the party accepted in word and deed that the Gorkhas would never find fulfillment except through self-rule. The document begins with the statement that 'The CPI(M) notes the democratic awakening among the Nepali-speaking people living in the hill regions of Darjeeling district and other *adjacent areas* (stress added) and appreciates their urge for their regional autonomy...It adheres to it and sincerely strives for the formation of regional autonomy for the Nepali-speaking people of Darjeeling and surrounding areas in West Bengal.' Surely there can be nothing more categorical than that. The document then explains how the party will go about creating this autonomy: 'The CPI(M) pledges that it will at the first opportunity introduce a bill in the West Bengal Assembly for constituting the autonomous region of Darjeeling in West Bengal State and setting up a Regional Council conferring on it all the necessary legislative and executive power, that are in conformity with the constitutional provisions and powers of the West Bengal State Government.'

The CPI(M) was conscious that Delhi could always block such a move. The answer? 'It will be necessary to overcome the obstacles by the struggle of the common people of West Bengal to compel the Government of India to make changes in the Constitution. It also assures the Nepali-speaking people of Darjeeling and adjacent areas that it will mobilize all other democratic parties and groups in the State in support of their legitimate rights for regional autonomy.' In other words, the CPI(M) assured the Gorkhas of a popular movement in support of autonomy if Delhi refused. As far as a change in the Constitution was concerned, that would be necessary too because while Article 244A permitted autonomy within the framework of a State, it only allowed this principle in relation to 'The Scheduled and Tribal Areas.' The Gorkhas are not, by their own claim, tribals.

The CPI(M) document then provided a detailed list of the authority that would be enjoyed by the elected Regional Council, voted to power through the 'principle of proportional representation.' The administration of the 'Darjeeling Autonomous Region shall be vested in the Executive...The Regional Council shall have powers to make laws on all subjects connected with the economic, social and cultural life of the people living in the region, and regarding internal administrative set-up'. Although it was indicated that this would have to be in conformity with the laws and enactments of West Bengal on a number of key matters, it would need a two-thirds majority in the West Bengal Assembly to overturn any law enacted by the Regional Council.

Most important, however, was the provision that all the administration would be in the Nepali language 'as an essential first step to associate the people in the exercise of their rights or autonomy' and the 'medium of instruction shall be Nepali language at all stages: with adequate provision for other minority language peoples.' With these two demands being granted, it would, in fact, make no material difference whether the region was considered a part of West Bengal or not. The State language had been reduced to a 'minority language.' And lastly: 'The Regional Council shall have the right to raise its own finances, by various taxes and budget it for its development. The State of West Bengal would provide additional grants, not merely those amounts which are specially sanctioned by the Central Government but also from its State resources keeping in view the necessity of making the people of this region enjoy the same economic and cultural standards as those in the other advanced areas of the State.' There was really nothing left to add. This commitment was made on behalf of the CPI(M) by Rattanlal Brahmin in 1970.

Nor did the CPI(M) go back on its word. It followed up its promise with action in the legislature. It took a little time to do so, since the CPI(M) only returned to power in 1977, but it introduced a resolution, dutifully passed in the West Bengal Assembly, first in 1978 and then in September 1981, demanding that the Centre grant regional autonomy to the three hill subdivisions and include Nepali in the Eight Schedule of the Constitution. The Centre, both in Morarji Desai's time and in Mrs Indira Gandhi's, rejected these resolutions as potentially divisive. But the CPI(M) refused to change its stance and continued to promote the line that the Gorkhas would not find genuine freedom without autonomy.

As recently as 1985, the CPI(M) Member of Parliament, Ananda Pathak (who was a worker of the party when the Darjeeling unit was first formed) moved a Constitution Amendment Bill (Number 122) for the granting of regional autonomy to the three hill subdivisions of Darjeeling with the consent of his party. The Bill was introduced on 9 August 1985 in the Lok Sabha and debated on three days, 6 December 1985, 21 February 1986 and 7 March 1986. Officially, this was a private member's Bill, but Left Front parties like the CPI and Revolutionary Socialist Party (RSP) also supported the Bill in addition to the CPI(M).

And this was not the first attempt: in 1982 Ananda Pathak, Samar Mukherjee and Somnath Chatterjee proposed Bill number 59 for the 'formation of an autonomous region comprising certain areas in West Bengal and creation of a District Council.'

The move in 1982 proved abortive without Congress encouragement, and the matter could have been left to lie there. In fact, the effort in 1985 was a little surprising, given all that had happened in Punjab, and the mood of the nation vis-a-vis anything that even vaguely smacked of separatism. It could hardly have been wise counsel which persuaded a CPI(M) MP to move such a Bill but it did happen.

Ananda Pathak, the CPI(M) member from Darjeeling, stood up in the Lok Sabha and made a speech which would have certainly worked had it been made before the creation of the Fazal Ali Commission (set up to create linguistic States), before the disintegration of the North-east into seven sisters, before the long and bloody battles in the Punjab, before the volatile language riots that rocked north and south, before the assassination of a Prime Minister in the cause of separatism. The demand for autonomy, in the hill areas, said Mr Pathak would strengthen 'the unity and integrity of the country' and cement the bond of brotherhood and friendship between the people of an isolated hill area situated on the 'extreme border and the people of the rest of India.' He rejected the idea that the call for autonomy was separatist or secessionist. He argued that the principle of autonomy had been accepted in the Constitution under Article 244, and that there were already a number of elected councils in Assam, Tripura, Meghalaya and Mizoram (Mr Pathak ignored the proviso that this could only be done in tribal areas). Mr Pathak continued to argue: 'You have to draw them (the Gorkhas) into the process of national integration and development and also allow them to play their role in this process of development and integration according to their own aptitude and characteristics. In other words, Mr Pathak was also alleging that the Gorkhas had not been able to enter the process of development and integration so far —he might have added that his constituency of Darjeeling, towards which the speech was aimed, had also been failed in this r-he might have added that his constituency of Darjeeling, towards which the speech was aimed, had also been failed in this respect by his own Left Front Government which had been in power in Bengal for the last ten years.

Mr Pathak continued to try and persuade the House. There had to be some sort of statehood, he said, and immediately quoted Jawaharlal Nehru's suggestion about a Scottish pattern of autonomy in these regions. Mr Pathak stressed that the Gorkhas had not been able to be on par with others, and they wanted to participate in 'national reconstruction' in their own way. Culturally, socially, economically, educationally and mentally they were different from the majority nationalities. Only money would not solve the problem — they would never feel like a 'real partner' in India without autonomy.

It was extremely eloquent. No Gorkha could have made a plea for separation from the control of Bengali-dominated Calcutta so well.

Mr Pathak then defined the consequences of not giving autonomy — secessionist demands would result out of frustration. Mr Pathak then told the House that the West Bengal Assembly had unanimously supported the demand, which is true and that the people of the State were totally for it, which, however, is a most doubtful proposition.

The Union Home Minister S.B. Chavan's answer seemed more conversant with the mood of the people: 'I can merely say that constitution of autonomous councils of legislature is fraught with all kinds of dangerous implications.' In retrospect this seems an obvious enough reply: the only surprise is that this did not occur to the CPI(M) when it was resurrecting this move to grant autonomy to Darjeeling district. From 1982 the exercise had been left in cold storage; and nothing much happened in Darjeeling. The idea had, in fact, been dormant for so long that no one really expected anything to come out of it immediately. It would be interesting to know whose bright idea it was to bring it to a head by another formal effort in the Lok Sabha to get it passed. Mr Chavan was unambigous in his assessment of the implio a head by another formal effort in the Lok Sabha to get it passed. Mr Chavan was unambigous in his assessment of the implications of the Bill: if autonomy were accepted today, tomorrow it would be statehood and then who could stop similar 'lands' everywhere else? 'There are very dangerous implications if we accept a proposal of this nature,' he pointed out. Mr Chavan in fact tried to dissuade Mr Pathak from introducing the Bill, saying that this would only be interpreted all over the country as another victory for separatist forces if it succeeded. But Mr Pathak, his eye concentrated on his own constituency rather than the country, went ahead. He did not even consider that Mr Chavan could and did accuse the Left Front Government of having contributed to the problem by doing nothing to bring the Gorkhas into the mainstream if indeed they were out of it. Mr Pathak did not realize that there was a strong element of self-indictment in the Bill; or, if he did, then he chose to ignore that too. Did the CPI(M) really think that there was any chance of Rajiv Gandhi supporting the Bill at any stage? Surely the party is not that naive. Then what was the rationale for raising the issue at that moment?

After a debate on three different days in December, February and March, the Bill came up for a vote and was duly rejected by 47 votes to 17. The CPI and the RSP supported the CPI(M) in the vote. The rest of the country did not notice very much; there was so much else to get excited about from Shah Bano to Punjab. But in Darjeeling they noticed. And people who had been kept out in the cold for long years, suddenly began to find an audience. Now that the demand for autonomy would never be accepted in the legislature, the time had come for action. The Congress would not accept this demand for autonomy, and the CPI(M) could not make it accept. The level of the message to the country had to change.

The Centre, whether in Congress hands or Janta, had always rejected this demand: if anything Morarji Desai was more acerbic than his succesors. Everyone understood, more so now, that acceptance would become the signal for a rash of similar demands all across the country. It is not, however, as if everyone in the Congress had taken this line: the Darjeeling unit of the Congress has long been sounding like the CPI(M) on this issue. But there were two differences, one comparatively minor, the other major. Instead of autonomy, the district Congress had demanded that Darjeeling be made a Union Territory. But this is minor since the end result is separation from Calcutta in either case; the local Congressmen tagged on to this option largely to sound different from the Communists. But the second point is more important. While the CPI(M) adopted this line at the party level, the Congress high command never allowed the proposal of its Darjeeling unit to become part of its formal policy.

March became a crucial month in the history of Darjeeling. Hardly had the message of the Bill's defeat reached than an incident took place in Meghalaya: the coincidence is interesting. And an obscure writer, who had been alternately an object of derision or indifference, was waiting. No one can protect you, he had been telling the Gorkhas, but me and you need protection, he added. But perhaps the most interesting aspect of the situation was that this less than intellectual writer had an excellent strategy mapped out, and quite enough to remain both liquid and mobile. Someone had told him about the ultimate camouflage in this unique subcontinent — a cloak of patriotism over secession.

The idea of autonomy, of separation from the Bengali, had travelled some distance from Rattanlal Brahmin, sliding through one ism after another. It had been seized by a man with a single dimension. In a few weeks the newest child of an old movement would send another shudder through an aching nation.

August 1986

The Tyranny of the Failed Artiste

*The man who spearheads the Gorkha separatist movement is a
retired soldier and a novelist of limited gifts. A profile of Subhas
Ghising.*

'It was midnight and all the birds and animals were asleep. In
the sky the moon played hide and seek with the clouds.
Wrapped in a blanket, Purnima lay crying. Through the
window moonlight fell on her face. It was exactly a month
today since she had been parted from Kamal. She told
herself over and over again that his letter would come today,
tomorrow or day after. She carried Kamal in her eyes, and
cried; her brother, sleeping in the same room, pretended not
to see. Tonight her heart was especially heavy...'

Having done absolutely nothing spectacular in his six years with
the Indian Army, Subhas Ghising first sought to achieve his
obviously powerful need for fame and recognition through writing
fiction. Five books were published, of which *Neelo Choli* (The
Blue Choli) became the most famous. As the quotation from this
literary effort proves, the writing was unrelieved trash. (One interesting strand that runs through the stories is that Gorkha women
tie up their men with bonds of romance and prevent them from
fulfilling a higher mission.) As history tells us, there are few greater
dangers than the failed artiste giving vent to his frustrated aggres-
sion through politics. He found a personal reason for anger too. In
1979, he was evicted from land which he had encroached upon. In
1980, Ghising started an organization called Neelo Jhanda, (Blue
Flag) and his first slogan to the Gorkhas was that they were
Nepalis and they must protect and preserve this identity. No one
took him seriously. But he was tireless and kept travelling from
village to village spreading his message, telling the people that they

were Gorkhas first, and supporters of the Communists — the CPI(M)-or the Congress second.

He attempted to organize a boycott of the 1984 Parliamentary elections using the slogan 'No State, no vote,' but no one listened. There was a partial boycott in only six polling booths, the highest being a twenty-five per cent no-show in Mirik (an area which is currently the most militant). But it was during this time that he came to the attention of the local administration, amid whispers that both the number of young people around him and the cash at his private disposal were growing. However, his rhetoric was still in search of a sufficient audience. The demand for autonomy and the inclusion of Nepali in the Eight Schedule* goes back a long time, and while the Gorkhas have given expression to their senti-ments when, occasion arose, they had never started a sustained movement. The most dramatic protest, in fact, took place in the Seventies when Indira Gandhi visited Darjeeling. Someone had, either mistakenly or mischievously, spread the word that Mrs Gandhi was going to announce the acceptance of Nepali as a national language, and the most massive crowd ever seen in the hill station gathered for her speech. When there was no mention of the language problem the crowd became restive and then violent. Police had to rescue the late Prime Minister from the dais and eventually ninety-nine companies of paramilitary forces had to be used to clear the virtual siege of Darjeeling. As for the visit of another Prime Minister, Morarji Desai was in a class of his own. When he came in 1979, he told the Gorkhas that if they wanted to go back to Nepal they were welcome to, but he was not going to concede anything. The Gorkhas were simply too stunned to react then but those words have come back to haunt the future.

Subhas Ghising does nothing without consulting an astrologer. In fact at any meeting where a crucial decision is being made, this astrologer is present and almost inevitably becomes the decision-maker. The astrologer must have told his novelist-politician friend that his stars were going to take a dramatic turn from March. A confluence of events and circumstances suddenly brought about the moment in which the writer of cheap romances could suddenly

*The Eighth Schedule of the Indian Constitution lists the national languages: Assamese, Bengali, Gujarati, Hindi, Kannada, Kashmiri, Malayalam, Marathi, Oriya, Punjabi, Sanskrit, Sindhi, Tamil, Telegu and Urdu.

take his cherished place in the limelight he had sought all his life. At one level, the victory of the Asom Gana Parishad (AGP) in Assam and the Akalis in the Punjab in 1985 had given impetus to the feeling that there was purchase in a long political movement, and that nothing would be achieved without such a movement. Second, with the installation of the AGP Government, pressure on Nepalis living in the North-east began to be applied, fuelling fears that their existence in India was under renewed threat — the implication being that they would never have true safety unless they had their own State. Third, the CPI(M) effort through the Private Member's Bill moved by the party MP from Darjeeling, Ananda Mohan Pathak, to provide autonomy to Darjeeling and adjacent Nepali areas came up for a final discussion in March and a vote which, of course, Mr Pathak lost.

Subhas Ghising could now claim that neither the Congress nor the CPI(M) was really interested in the Gorkhas, that these were just games meant to deceive. And then came the most fortuitous incident, at least for Ghising. More than a thousand Nepalis working in the coal mines of Meghalaya were suddenly and arbitrarily picked up, dumped into trucks and pushed into Assam. Assam forwarded them to Bengal. The Bengal Government, which had taken care of the Bengali refugees from Assam when they turned up, simply ignored the Nepalis, who eventually had to find their way back across the unguarded border to Nepal. Ghising could now say, with a certain degree of triumph: 'I told you so.'

And all the exaggerations suddenly became Biblical truth. More than Rs.200 lakh worth of tea belonging to the Gorkhas was being stolen each year by the Bengalis of Calcutta, Ghising roared, and they all believed. The timber that could make every Gorkha rich was being taken away by the Bengalis, Ghising roared, and they all believed. When Gorkhaland was born and the Bengalis driven away, every Gorkha boy would get a job, Ghising roared, and they all believed. When Gorkhaland had its own police force, every Gorkha who was a constable would become an inspector, Ghising roared, and the constables believed (which is why most administration plans for action are leaked to the Gorkha National Liberation Front (GNLF) well in advance).

Perhaps the most dangerous thing that Ghising is doing is trying similar tactics with the Army. His message to the jawans in the

Indian Army is: what is the maximum that they can end up as? Havildar (an NCO), at best. He cites his own example. But in the future 40,000-strong Gorkhaland army they would all be officers. At such moments Ghising forgets that his official strategy is to sound more patriotic than thou, and win his separate State through the clever route of patriotism, but being a man of distinctly limited abilities he tends to occasionally forget his own cleverness.

Intellectuals, in fact, arc a bugbear to him. At one meeting he told his audience that they, and not those who had gone to school and college, were the real intellectuals. How was that? Simple. They had come to listen to him, and they had understood him. The so-called educated group had not come to listen, so they could never understand what he was saying. So who was the real intellectual? Those who understood him or those who did not? QED.

The trouble with this propaganda is not that it is foolish, but that it is working. As we have seen, the Communists have done enough to convince even those who might have had any doubts that the Gorkha was so different that he would never find true development and identity in a Bengali-majority State without autonomy. On top of this is a typical, long list of real grievances. The traditional image of the plains babu coming to the hills in search of pleasure, with its implications of exploitation of women, is still a dominant part of the Gorkha consciousness. (The incident which could spark off more violence than anything else is if there is any case of the paramilitary police misbehaving with local girls.) On top of that are complaints about the neglect of social services (electricity and water obviously being the most common), about the denudation of forests, about discrimination in employment, about the neglect of the Nepali language.

The Chief Minister of West Bengal, Jyoti Basu, has his replies: the per capital expenditure by the State Government on Darjeeling is double that spent on other districts; the per capita income of Darjeeling is the fourth highest. But the Gorkha is not in any mood to believe the Bengali, not even Jyoti Basu. The graffiti on the walls reflects his new attitude: 'Bengal must stop looting us...We are not slaves of Bengal...Bengal is not our master.' And in the developing tourist resort of Mirik, Gorkhaland has already been declared. The notice in front of the beautiful lake there, put up by the

Fisheries Department of the State Government, no longer has Government of West Bengal painted on it — it says Government of Gorkhaland. Local residents of this region are the most militant and, according to some reports, trying to seize control from Ghising on the grounds that he is too moderate! They have simply changed the notice board. In a way it is fortunate that there are no tourists around.

The dream has been given specific contours. The green flag (much to the consternation of the spluttering sahibs of the planters' club, it resembles their standard) of the GNLF flutters from housetop and shop in Darjeeling, emblazoned with a *kukri*, three stars and four stripes. They have delineated the capitals: permanent capital, Darjeeling; winter capital, Cooch Behar; the business capital, Siliguri; and the cultural capital, Kalimpong. In anxious whispers around Ghising they discuss other demands for separation and pray for their success so that the country becomes a conglomeration of 'lands' and 'sthans', each doubtless with its 40,000 strong army and quickly escalating defence budget. There is encouragement from known and unknown sources: the political pot in the hills must be kept boiling. Clause 7 of the Indo-Nepal Agreement* is turned into an effective bogey. Passions must be kept high by drama; Gorkhas are notorious for their quicksilver attitudes, at an impossible high when stirred to assault, but easily depressed and ineffective in a sustained battle. And so there will be one movement after another in this opera of puppets — a *bandh*, a ceremonial burning, a programme to stop the transfer of timber. And each time victory will be declared, no matter what really happens: who can argue that a gesture has been defeated.

It will be a slogging match. And the Government must be prepared to use a mix of balm and punitive measures to send the message that while doors will remain open, instigators will not be allowed licence. There is no need to create martyrs; but there is need to stress that the advantages of assimilation cannot be taken for granted by those who work for secession. The Gorkha National

*Article 7 of the treaty of peace and friendship between the Government of India and Nepal (1950) says: 'The Government of India and Nepal agree to grants on a reciprocal basis, to the nationals of one country in the territories of the other some privileges in the matter of residence, ownership of property, participation in trade and commerce, movement and other privileges of a similar nature.'

Liberation Front, an object of derision just a few months ago, has become a chapter in our history in the last few weeks. But the time has come to peel away the layers of hypocrisy and ask — what liberation are you talking about? Which kind of national do you really want to be?

It is not rational argument which is going to persuade Subhas Ghising and his supporters now. They have set a spirit abroad — of separation — and they are in the heady process of dreaming. They are convinced that the country is fragile at the moment, that its abilities have been shaken by the debilitating violence in the west and the east, and the moment has come to unfurl another banner. They are confident that the threat of violence and economic disruption will be sufficient to force concessions from Calcutta and Delhi. They are waiting to exploit the contradictions inherent in a democracy — separate party interests — to further their cause.

Subhas Ghising began his present incarnation as a novelist. No matter, his politics is still a short story. It can be kept at this level with some administrative ability and a lot of political wisdom. The first is available: north Bengal has extremely good bureaucrats in place. The second should not be beyond the imagination of the CPI(M) and the Congress(I). Punjab was ruined because political parties could never quite draw the line between their interests and the national interest. Surely the same mistake can be avoided. The CPI(M) and the Congress have declared their desire to forget the past, particularly their own, and concentrate on the future. And only if the future can be protected from the mistakes of the past, will it be truly safe.

August 1986

Meerut's Politics of Communalism

One of the most bestial crimes committed in recent years was the coldblooded massacre of innocent Muslims by the Provincial Armed Constabulary (PAC) in Meerut. Nevertheless, U.P Chief Minister, V.B. Singh, came down heavily on the side of the PAC, and tried to exonerate the force of apreceded this brutality were fanned by men with dangerous ambitions, manipulators using human beings as fodder.

This is the same story that one wrote from Jamshedpur and Ayodhya and Moradabad and anywhere else. Two communities start a slow pirouette of confrontation which gradually builds up to the moment when the tension must explode into violence. Then the beat of a drum near a mosque, or a stone thrown on a procession, or a knife slipped into the side of a stranger in the darkness of the night. The frenzy of battle, and then a rogue section of the police takes side, presiding over murder, loot and worse to teach these *sala Pakistanis* a lesson, amidst the familiar echoes in the background of treachery and sinister motive. Passion spent, the frenzy abates: the sanc clements of the State machinery reassert themselves, the rogues are brought under some control, relief is distributed amid the familiar complaints of discrimination. Rumour and the anger of revenge keep hearts simmering, and only slowly, very slowly, do the living stop che dead. All that remains at the end is memory: the clutching sob mother unable to understand why her twenty-five-year-old son is dehen hc was living yesterday, and the liquid sparkle of an old father's near blind eyes, bearing a permanent pool of tears, which will neither course down the white stubble on a dark face or go back to the wells inside his heart from which they sprang.

But news is often nothing but the latest twist in an old tale. So, for better or for worse, read how the bodies from the town of Meerut were found floating down the Hindon canal.

The silhouette is easily recognizable despite the drapes, but the statue of the last Prime Minister at the Indira Chowk remains unveiled because the official ceremony has not been organized yet. The high street curves at the *chowk* towards the Gulshan Cinema on one side and a new and rather pretty mosque on the other. Small lanes, like quicksilver rivulets, run off from the main road, and in these lanes survive, as best as they can, those who serve the needs of the middle class and the poor: the weavers and lower income wage earners. It is appropriate that the colony of Bihari Ansari weavers called Hashimpura should be near the Indira Gandhi Chowk, because it was during her memorable 1969-71 phase that they were first given the loans and the concessions which helped these weavers to reach the status which is best described in Hindi: 'Khaata-Peeta.' (Earning enough to eat). It was the welfare programmes of those days which rescued this particular lot from destitution. They have pukka houses now, each with its set of looms on which the family works to earn its livelihood.

Abdul Majid's house is atypical for only one reason: there is a very beautiful neem tree rising at the centre of the courtyard. The old man and his wife were not particularly upset when the Provincial Armed Constabulary came to their house at five that Friday afternoon: after all, they were doing the same search in every Muslim house along this lane. They told the police they would sit near the tree while they looked wherever they wanted: there was nothing to find, in any case, in the two dark rooms of the house. In the end, the only thing which the police could find in this home was a young man, the son, Din Mohammad, in his early twenties, and the principal breadearner of the family. They accepted their fate when the son was arrested. Once again, virtually every able bodied young man in the lane was taken away as a potential or actual rioter.

When six nights later, on 28 May 1987, the police came to Abdul Majid's house and told him that his son in jail was anxious to meet his father, they could barely understand this spasm of generosity; there was a tinge of anxiety, the fear that their son might be in pain after torture. They reached the jail at around nine that night. It was also the night of the Id moon, the happiest evening in the Muslim's calendar, but thoughts of a celebration were far away as the old man waited for the police to let him know what fate they had in store for him. He learnt the truth finally at around 2.30 in the morning. His son Din Mohammad was dead. And the father had only been called to take away the body and bury it before dawn. The orders were strict: they had to bury the body right away, before Id the next day, and a grave had even been dug. As best as he could, Abdul Majid, with the help of a friend who had come with him, offered the last prayers and interred the putrefying body of his son in the darkness. He was not alone. There were three other fathers come to bury bodies that night.

These four Muslim youths were not victims of riots but of coldblooded murder by the police in the lock-up.

The district authorities have now given up trying to deny these four deaths. In answer to how, the police say they have no explanation. And the civil service administrator for Meerut airily waves away charges of discrimination by saying that it is always the administration, is it not, which becomes the goat in such matters (it slipped his burdened memory that the word is scapegoat, but no matter).

*

A fear and horror is running through the Muslims of Meerut that such deaths in police custody could be substantial. More and more gruesome reports are surfacing about how the brutal and communal force known as the PAC has been taking its revenge on Muslims.

More than two dozen young Muslims were picked up from the Hashimpura area by the PAC on the bank of the Hindon canal in Ghaziabad that night, shot dead and dumped into the water where their bodies floated down-stream till they were fished out next morning. And it might never have been known that these men had died at the hands of the Provincial Armed Constabulary rather than in communal clashes were it not for a miracle. Two of those young men who were shot and thrown into the canal survived. Mujibur Rahman and Badruddin (whose relatives were in Hashimpura when we visited it) were shot in the chest and thrown into the canal, but they did not die. When the Muradnagar police picked them up ten kilometres downstream they were still breathing. In the Narinder Mohan hospital under heavy security, they still had breath enough to narrate their awful story.

Who knows how many became victims of the PAC that night.

The administration says calmly that 2,568 people were picked up from about seventy *mohallas*. Is that the figure which was picked up or only the number which was finally lodged in a number of jails dotted across Uttar Pradesh from Agra to Fatehgarh (which is 400 kilometres from Meerut)?

The riots, and the toll they extracted, were indescribably bad, but perhaps nothing compared to the arbitrary murder committed by the PAC.

There is a point beyond which it is impossible, at least for me, to describe death: you have to leave it as a statistic and be done with it. And though it is far from adequate, the only available answer we have for crime is punishment. It may not bring back the dead, but it does become a message for the living. In the first wave of revulsion, after news of the PAC's behaviour spread, there was talk that the superintendent had been suspended, that the PAC might be withdrawn. Only days later, the gestures were heavily diluted. Because the Provincial Armed Constabulary had become the hero of the Hindus. One slogan which greeted Rajiv Gandhi continually during his visit to Meerut on Saturday was *PAC zindabad*. On the morning of 31 May as we were walking through the deserted, curfew-struck streets of Meerut, we met a khadi-wearing chief warden who described himself as a Congressman doing his duty for the nation in these arduous times. There was one thing which we must never forget to write, he said. 'Everyone in Meerut wants the PAC to stay.' He insisted, 'Ask anyone.' Had it not been for the fact that the Prime Minister decided to drive himself and stopped wherever he noticed groups of Muslims on the streets, he would have returned to Delhi with only the orchestrated part of the story.

The truth about a communal riot has so many shades that it is rarely possible to define anything in black and white. As far as the battles between the people were concerned, there was enough guilt on both sides, the Muslim no less than the Hindu. But the partisanship of the involved people is to be expected: that, after all, is why the riots began in the first place. It is when the so-called guardians turn into communal armies that order begins to crumble. To allow guilty police to escape is to condone a police state. And the consequences of that will be far, far larger than just death in Meerut.

*

Salim Ahmed Ansari loves the alias he himself has promoted: he is known in Meerut as Salim *urf* (the Urdu for alias) Bhindranwale. Around 40 years of age, he edged his way into politics through the Muslim Youth Conference organized by Javed Habib. When the Babari Masjid issue came up, he at once hitched his wagon to this cause. His road to ' salvation' for Muslims, repeated in conversation after conversation with the city's youth, was, *'larhna, marna hai.'* (We will fight and die) And he would butress this line with the example of Punjab: *'Ek karor sardar hain, aur yeh to samhal nahin rahe Rajiv Gandhi sey, ham 20 karor hain, hamen kaise samhalega?* (There are one crore Sikhs, and Rajiv Gandhi cannot tackle them. how will he tackle 20 crore Muslims?)' The accuracy of the figures is not the point, the direction of the message is. Other, more famous, Muslim leaders of this ilk have been giving their support to such preaching. Ansari organized a meeting of the Hyderabad MP Salahuddin Owaisi, and Owaisi's message to the Muslims of Meerut was: *'Takkat paida karo. Taakat maa ke qaatilon se samjhauta karwa deti hai* (Build your strength. It is strength which creates a settlement with the killers of your mother).' It does not take much intelligence to appreciate the reference points.

The new politics of these modern extremists is actually an echo of the old Muslim League politics: turn nationalism into a bargaining point. Threaten the State with revolt in order to win your demands. And arm yourself to prove how strong you can be.

This provocative challenge to India was given a kind of formal status at the Boat Club rally in Delhi in support of the Babari Masjid demands. There is no proper understanding yet of the impact the speeches made there have had on excitable Muslims, particularly the youth. Meerut, being a town close to Delhi, sent thousands to that rally. Imam Bukhari's speech there, declaring that this country could not be called a legitimate home of the Muslims, has been reported, but not the more dangerous speech of Syed Shahabuddin.

I have a video cassette of that speech, and the implicit and explicit call to violence that exists there has to be heard to be believed. Syed Shahabuddin warned India of the 'consequences' of Muslim anger.

The reason why Shahabuddin is more dangerous than the Imam is because he provides the legitimacy of a respectable politician to these provocative arguments. When the Imam says all this, well he is a loudmouth extremist even when everyone from H.N.Bahuguna to Mrs Indira Gandhi kept tripping over one other to purchase his support. But Shahabuddin represents what secular Indian Muslim leadership should be all about: his career in the foreign service was interrupted when eminent leaders like Atal Behari Vajpayee and Chandra Shekhar brought him to politics to become the Muslim leader of the Janata ranks. Today, he is an important spokesman of the Janta Party, and not the Muslim League. And if a senior Janta MP can give a barely disguised call for insurrection, then why blame the Muslim youth in a depressed *mohalla* for believing that perhaps there is no answer except violence? And if upstarts parading themselves as Muslim Bhindranwales find patronage from the Babari Masjid committee (whose most famous member is Shahabuddin), then what justice is there in picking up a poor and frustrated young man from a *mohalla* like Hashimpura and condemning him as an antisocial and antinational element?

For the last two years, and in particular after the Babari Masjid controversy, this message of salvation through confrontation has been drilled into the Muslim mind in *mohalla* after *mohalla*, through small meetings and large, addressed by extremist leaders minor and major. A whirlwind was being deliberately sown, and we have begun reaping it. Opposition parties like the Janata condoned it because they were convinced that only Rajiv Gandhi would suffer (although the one Janata Chief Minister, Ramakrishna Hegde, was wise enough not to allow his own party MP Shahabuddin to hold meetings in Bangalore).

There is great political profit in death of course. Those who light the fires typically run away from the arson: Salim Ansari has spent the whole period of the Meerut riots in Delhi. Imam Bukhari can take comfort in the fact that the administration did not allow him to enter Meerut. Shahabuddin went for a couple of hours, and extracted every ounce of publicity with photographs sent to the newspapers (for some unknown reason Shahabuddin was laughing in the picture: no one has understood what there was or is to laugh about).

The tactic is a transparent one: build up passions, and provoke the community to the point of riots which, when they come, will justify your original call for militancy.

And it is these leaders like Imam Bukhari and Syed Shahabuddin who have given fresh currency to the charge of antinationalism. That there is a powerful section within India always ready to hammer Muslims with the Partition stick is not a secret. But this belief is spreading today, thanks to the speeches being made by the most prominent leaders of the Muslim community. The problem is accentuated by the fact that the traditional political machinery in small towns has been replaced these days by an aggressive lumpen element eager to fill the vacuum.

We have reached then a circle of vicious and horrible distress: on the one side political parties like the Janata giving legitimacy to leaders like Shahabuddin, and on the other criminal and communal forces like the PAC using this excuse to indulge in the massacre of innocents. And in the process, the people are getting communalized as never before. There is no Congress and Janata and Lok Dal during riots in Meerut, there is only Hindu and Muslim. Even so-called 'leftist' Congress leaders of Meerut have become great devotees of the PAC.

And the man who has used the anit-national stick against Muslims in Meerut is Vir Bahahdur Singh, the Chief Minister of Uttar Pradesh. Even when Rajiv Gandhi came to Meerut, V.B.Singh organized demonstrations in favour of the PAC, and even as non-controversial a leader as Mrs Mohsina Kidwai was insulted and abused with the tacit consent of the Chief Minister.

All through, the administration in Meerut has adopted an anti-Muslim attitude. And if there was any more evidence needed to prove the point then it came with the transfer of two senior police officers who had a reputaiton for integrity, V.K.B. Nair and Nathu Lal. The officers who allowed or participated in brutality of the most horrendous kind are being protected by the State administration. And the line is being spread that it was the Muslims who were the real aggressors.

There is truth in the charge that it was the Muslims who first provoked the riots: 'inspired' by the Bukhari-Shahabuddin loyalists, they began the trouble on the 18th of May. But after that the revenge has been severe. The police and the PAC even indulged in arbitrary killing. There was Maliana, the village out side Meerut. And today survivors are talking of a figure of around 200 dead in one incident alone near the Hindon canal.

These weavers from Hashimpura became the '*sala Pakistanis*' whom the PAC sent to their death in cold blood, all pawns in a game being played for stakes as high as power. Votes are being counted in terms of corpses, and by every player—both the Shahabuddins and the Vir Bahadur Singhs. After forty years, our nation's acceptability level for murder and mayhem has risen to unprecedented levels: that is one of the 'achievements' of our system. And yet there comes a point when the reddened mind must demand a halt, and accountability.

Imam Bukhari can perhaps be left alone in the petty world he has created. But at least leaders who claim that they feel a sense of responsibility towards the country must take action: Chandra Shekhar against his communal lieutenant Syed Shahabuddin, and Rajiv Gandhi against his communal Chief Minister, Vir Bahadur Singh. That will not solve the problem, which is already a monster much larger than its progenitors. But it will be a very small beginning towards that end.

June 1987

Life and Death on a Burning Ghat

The dom, who disposed of the dead, lives in a macabre world of his own. Despised by everyone, he drowns his sorrows in hard liquor and in hallucinatory dreams produced by ganja *(marijuana). An exploration of the squalid existence of those who live among the dregs of humanity.*

Nimtollah: The river gives and the river takes away, and perfectly logically, we pray to our different forms of sustenance.

On Shuklapanchami, of the month of Magha, five days after the birth of the waxing moon, Calcutta bows to Saraswati: to the river of knowledge, to Nadi, the banks of which inspire scholarship, poetry and the hymns that probe beyond the reaches of the philosopher's imagination. She is Vakdevi, the goddess of the word, the beginning of life in its higher form; she is Jyotirmayi, spreading the light of thought and wis*dom*. She is the wife of Brahma, (the creator), fair, with her hands she creates the music of the *veena*, she sits on the pure swan, there are flowers in her hair and she is dressed in white. Krishna, the Dark One, craved for her. She is beautiful, Vishalakshmi, the large-eyed goddess, and the Brahmin gives her life each year in the month of Magha by taking *surma* (kohl) and *kaajal* from the leaf of a wood apple and applying it to her eyes and touching her cheeks. O fair lady, on whose forehead the young moon dwells, seated on a white lotus, a pen in one hand and a book in the other, we look towards you, O goddess of utterance, for our good fortune, pray those who crave the magic of learning, those who want from the river Saraswati more than fertility for the land, those who want civilization and the fertility of the mind. Saraswati is the goddess of the school and the middle class, the children of literacy in all its uneven variety, stretching from the clerk's numerals to the scholar's erudition. Hail to thee Saraswati, the lotus-eyed , large-eyed, give us enlightenment. All around, in every book, the image of Saraswati is being worshipped; the *pandals* are up; twinkling clowns with folded hands, before and beyond an Air India maharajah, in a straight line, welcome you to one large *pandal* near Liberty cinema; smaller pujas are less exuberant but no less interesting as Calcutta uses another opportunity to display middle class creativity. The loudspeakers take you through the retinue of Bombay's latest music, and the young men and women have taken to the streets to see as many images as their legs allow and flirt as much as their hearts choose. But cross the train tracks that divide the city from Strand Road and Nimtollah ghat and Saraswati disappears. The *dom* prefers the god of death. After all, education to one is what death is to the other: a source of income.

The corpse is his life, and he worships the God of Ghosts and Spirits, Bhoot Nath, grey, nearly faceless, as is proper for the god from the dark side of Shiva. More than 150 years ago, the ancestors of the family of untouchables who still burn the dead at Nimtollah ghat, the Malliks, Gokul and Kanchan, came to a *peepul* tree on this spot on the bank of the Hooghly. Because they adopted Vaishnavism, they changed their surname from Mallik to Das, and their ash-streaked faces soon made them *mahatmas*. They were joined by Lal Baba, the red cloth around his loins giving him the appellation, and together they placed the stone that eventually grew into today's temple. Around the temple of Bhoot Nath came the bodies to be burnt, and the *doms* were in charge of both, the worship and the cremation. Then one day a Seth, frightened of the power of Bhoot Nath, sought to appease the god by building a tin shed around the image and painting it green. The collections increased. The Hindu Sanskar Samity began to get worried about this unusual phenomenon, a temple in the control of untouchables, and one, moreover, which had begun to get a clientele: after all, who was going to take a risk with the God of Ghosts, knowing full well that one would have to spend a much longer time in that state than in flesh and blood. And a god who could be bought off with offering and sacrifice would get his due, no matter if his self appointed representative was an untouchable fit only for the unclean functions of existence. Indu Bhushan of the Hindu Sanskar Samity decided to square this circle. A trust was set up, the *doms* were thrown out of the temple, proper Brahmins brought to fulfil their duty of prayer, and the house of the God of Ghosts was given plaster. And the collections naturally went to the trust. The *doms* however could keep what they got from their proper duty — the last extortion from the dead.

There is just one reminder of the past. The *aarti* worship is only done with cinders from the burning ghat; the God of Ghosts needs the fire of the dead.

*

The first to die was Manki Singh. He went at about seven on Monday morning. Ten minutes later it was Lalji Doodhwala. Nobody yet had caught the connection. Their deaths were too quick, too sudden, too much like the known arbitrariness of nature: when man wants to murder, he schemes and plans and bides the moment when he can swoop to kill, he is never arbitrary except by mistake. A little before eight on Monday morning, Joginder Mallik began to feel his nerves tighten, his body begin to stretch taut inside as if being pulled by some internal core that would implode his being.

His relatives all — the *doms* at Nimtollah are related: they are not going to hand over this control over the corpse to any outsider — thought that this was just another case of being possessed by a spirit. They were not too worried. They called Ram Chander Mallik, the cousin who talks to spirits: he spoke out the mantra and offered his diagnosis — there was no *bhoot* (ghost) within Joginder, his problem lay elsewhere. It was then that they asked him, and Joginder, between gasps, told them that he had gone out for a drink to Mama's homebrewn liquor shop the previous evening. They now got into a taxi and rushed to Medical College. The doctors made an effort but Joginder died by four in the afternoon. At night Khokhan Mukherjee died too. All of them had been destroyed by the poison in Mama's cheap liquor, consumed in his shack in the *gali* behind the teashop the previous night. The pity was that Mama was very well liked in the area. Everyone went to Santosh Mama's adda. You saw the death list, both a *dom* and a Mukherjee were on it. There is nothing like a city liquor joint to destroy *chooth chaath* (untouchability); who knows who has drunk from which glass? In our village Samastipur, Bihar, yes, twelve annas' worth of untouchability remains. What is your name, they ask. Mallik? Okay, get your own glass. But in a Calcutta shop...And Santosh Mama had been around for nearly twelve years and there never had been even a hint of trouble. God knows who brewed his liquor this time.

'Excuse me, you aren't from the police, are you? I mean there won't be any trouble, will there? I don't want any trouble, I don't know where he lives, so there is no point asking me!'

'No, no, I'm from the press, I told your friend where I came from.'

'Oh, a reporter. Which press?'

'An English newspaper.'

'English...English! That is the real paper; everybody reads the English paper. You must mention the telephone it has been out of order...'

'I was asking about the man who conversed with the *bhoot*...'

'Oh, so you don't believe in ghosts. I never did too. You know I have studied up to high school. I know how to read, so I did not believe what the elders had told me about the spirits. Let me tell you how I became a Believer.'

Babeswar Mallik was proud not only of his reading, but also of the comfortable roll of flesh around his stomach. That was not obesity, it was a mark of prosperity, a valuable symbol in a community where food had to be scrounged from the ashes. He was not at the mercy of the dead: he always had had a job. And it was while he was reading a Hindi novel called *Nagin* by Khushwant Kant, a tale so gripping that he could not put the book down even though it was long past midnight, that he saw his first ghost. They were building an electric crematorium then, in 1980 he thinks it was, and he was the contractor's guard, ensuring that his *dom* brethren did not steal any construction material. The bathroom was behind his head, and he heard steps from that side. He ignored them. Suddenly, two minutes later, he felt weak and drained, as if the strength had left his body totally. His first reaction was that he had been paralysed, and he remembered preferring death to paralysis, he did not want ever to be cleaned by another person. And then over his head, in front of his eyes, a hand appeared, and its fingernails kept growing. He started reciting in his mind the *Hanuman Chalisa* and when he had finished it, the shadow quickly withdrew. He turned and saw a human form disappear into the bathroom. By then he had recovered and he gave chase, and opened the bathroom door. There was no one inside.

If that was traditional, then hear this one. A story with most unusual qualities. This is the Tale of the Ghost Who Was a Trade Unionist. There is a moral in this story. Maybe, in fact, more than one moral.

The Oppressor was the owner of a factory making singlets: we shall not take his name out of respect for the rich and fear of libel. The day he was brought to the temple of Baba Bhoot Nath beside the crematorium, was also a day on which a prominent doctor had died. The doctors, who quickly learnt of our Oppressor's identity, sneered at him; this was only a case of epilepsy, what were rational people like him doing here, searching for an *ojha* (exorcist) who could communicate with the ghost who had seized this man?!

Sankı Baba, the *ojha*, took the leaf of *tulsi*, a stick of *dhoop kapur* (incense), and a garland of flowers and then began reciting his *mantra* to awaken the spirit. A crowd gathered. The factory owner's eyes turned large and blood-red as the ghost manifested himself. 'Who are you?' asked Sanki Baba. The ghost was frank. 'I am Santosh Biswas,' he replied. 'I used to work in this man's factory. I died in an accident there. This man has paid my wife three hundred rupees as compensation for the accident but he has not given her the three months' salary which are due to me. When she went to ask him for the money, he tried to seduce her. She refused so he stopped the money. All my life he has oppressed me. Now he is oppressing my wife, I will not leave him.'

The Baba offered terms to the Ghost of Mr Biswas. A deal was made. The spirit would leave the owner's body for five thousand rupees' cash, to be paid to the wife.

Two months later, the owner was back. Sanki *ojha* checked with the ghost. He was even more angry. The money had not been given. He wanted ten thousand rupees now, and then and there. The owner's wife had about Rs. 8,000 worth of jewels, which she offered, and about two thousand rupees were brought from their house. It was nine at night before the full sum was handed over to the wife. The factory owner has not come back to Nimtollah ghat after that.

Sneer if you like. After all, we are the children of Saraswati, who taught us to believe in her but not in Baba Bhoot Nath. We know reading 'riting and 'rithmetic. Baleswar Mallik, who tried to travel some distance towards us, learning how to read and abjuring superstition, has gone back to Baba Bhoot Nath. He believes in ghosts.

*

The first structure as you come to the ghat is a closed hall which ladies can use to change and descend to the river for their holy bath. Under the sculpture of the Goddess Ganga on a fish is a sign which makes it clear that men would be unwelcome inside. Next comes the Singha Dwar, the Gate of Lions, through which the dead must pass for the final touch of fire: do not be afraid, is that message. A clang of the bell, the stretch of shoes and slippers outside, the cool of a constantly washed floor, a place prominently listing the important trustees, the sound of *bhajans*: this is the new Temple of Baba Bhoot Nath, a devotee of Shiva, once just the god of the *doms* but now much higher on the rungs of respectability. There are stalls selling flowers, and shops selling *ganja*, and a medley of pavement businessmen hawking an imaginative range of wares but concentrating on the *chilam*. Beggars and *bhadralok* (gentleman). Welldressed men sitting on the bench of a poor man's teashop, waiting for a relative to burn.

Against the barbed wire stretched across wooden poles, the backdrop the huge British-red wall of the Saheb Bazar Railway Goods Office, are the shacks of the pitifully poor (there are, of course, degrees of poverty just as there are degrees of wealth), made of tattered and torn straw mats; the men and women are in hysterical conversation with one another, alternating between abuse, anger, near violence, then suddenly calming down to matter-of-fact conversation; the children have taught themselves very early to be oblivious; and, as I stand there watching, four of them, girls, place their arms around one another's neck to form a lovely knit and march down the Strand Road, giggling and singing, the harmony of a child's joy making exquisite music. The *ganja* shop has covered its walls with bright paintings of Shiva and scenes from his turbulent life, while in one corner Ganesh smiles serenely with his consort. Two men sit on their haunches on the river bank, talking to each other with heads bowed, their *chadars* half covering their heads: '*Aurat ka jaat...*' says one in an unfinished sentence which needs no finishing, and the other nods his head sagely, having understood perfectly. The Bihari in the middle of the crowd is singing Bhojpuri folk songs. This is a holiday, Saraswati Puja for others, and this is the evening's fun, singing with friends, one on a *dholak* (drum), another with *khol* and *kartals* (drums and cymbals). He twirls one corner of his moustache as he pauses, then with a dramatic flourish throws away a little of the tea in the *kulia* (small earthen cup) in front of him, gulps the rest, wipes his mouth with a swagger, and then resumes: *Shyam bajaaye beena, Ik din saawan ho...* Today is also the first day of spring, Basant. A young man in the crowd can't take it, the memory of his village in Bihar saddens him; '*Apna des aaj jor se phagua hoga heeya ka hai*? (Today there will be colour in my home, what is there here?). The singers are losing themselves, returning to their villages of Bihar, in the intoxication of an ever-faster beat. The *chilam* of *ganja* is passed around in the circle of friends sitting just around them. The lights come on at 5.40 in the evening. They are modern yellow, the generation beyond neon, soothing and powerful, not white and harsh. The moon, a single horn, the crescent of Shiva, shifts the grey sheet of cloud just a little, registers its presence, and then goes back behind the thin curtain. The colour of the world has changed in the last hour as the day melts into night, but the cloud insists on remaining dreary and depressing. The embankment is littered with chipped, mud tea cups. The lights on the mills across the river glow brighter in the growing dark and their self-reflecting images in the water travel deeper. A steamer approaches the jetty, one green light on the left, a red one on its right and a white light at the top. It honks as it nears harbour, and the sound is that of the rubber tube trumpet in old lorries. A tired *sadhu* relaxes under the spell of *ganja*, though his trident remains steady. On the steps leading down to the river little cups of fire light up; the *ganja* smokers (just you and I, with a little less money) are getting their chilams ready, or inhaling so deeply that the dormant fire in the cup gets a new life. The bustle on the road, in the temple, at the crematorium, at the teashops is high and the sound of *Hari Bol* as another body approaches is lost, or when not lost, just ignored.

*

The telephone. Lest we forget. Two years ago, the specially placed
public telephone of the Nimtollah ghat, put there in the service of
the bereaved, and the tragedy stricken, stopped working. The
office is there, as is the blue notice board, quite visible as a gesture
of modernity in the midst of an environment which seems as if it
has not changed for a hundred years. But the telephone does not
work. Actually no one misses it, except for a few of the more
confident *doms*, like Baleswar Mallik. What is the bigger problem
is that the water tap has broken down for one year, and the
Corporation man keeps coming occasionally to shake his head but
does nothing except return to shake his head once more. A beggar
sitting at his allotted place against the barbed wire pipes up:
perhaps he feels I have come to note complaints. His real problem
is that there is no latrine, not a single one: what should a beggar
like him do?

They are all waiting, waiting for the 21st century. Maybe they
will get a tap by then.

*

Manmohan Nath Bag was his name. It was an impressive name for
a beggar, and he himself rolled it around his tongue as he virtually
read it out, hinting that he had had an identity better than the
beggary he had been reduced to. I took the hint and asked.

He had come fifteen years ago from his village in Hooghly,
Chanditala. Fifteen years ago, his stomach had gone out of con-
trol, and then he fell down and broke his hand, and he could not
earn his living as a labourer anymore. Surely he had sons, a family.
He turned his face away, and the old man beside him answered,
'His son threw him out.'

'Most of us are here because our sons threw us out. The trouble
with us beggars,' the old man with a cackle said, 'is that we don't
die quickly enough. Otherwise our problem would be solved. We
have to end on that pyre across the street, so our children send us a
little ahead.' Another cackle.

Manmohan Bag turned his head away. He did not want to talk
about, or hear about, sons. He still loved the son who had thrown

him out.

'They would starve if it were not for the rich *seths* who come to Baba Bhoot Nath *mandir*,' said a bystander. 'They don't get much by way of alms. But they get *jilebi* and *puri*, or *bhaat* or something every day...' Than our commentator-friend turned satirical. "These *seths*. They steal the whole day and then come to Baba Bhoot Nath in the evening '*Maaf karo, Baba*: Forgive us, Baba. Will you forgive me my day's cheating if I give this poor man *jilebi*?'" Manmohan Nath Bag still wanted to assert some long-lost pride. 'I don't sleep here,' he told me. 'I stay here till the *seths* finish their *puja*, I eat, and then I go away to Katghora to sleep. I stay at Katghora,' he repeated, stressing the difference of his status from the rest of the seekers.

'Ah well,' I suggested, 'at least to sleep would be peaceful after a meal of *jilebi* and a drag of *ganja*'. He made a face. 'You know what they charge these days? One rupee for one *chutki* (a pinch).' It is, though, still within the reach of those without a single thing they can call their own, a single possession they can leave behind after death.

The old name of the approach road to Nimtollah Street and Nimtollah ghat was Ganja Gali. For all anyone knows or cares this may be the new name too.

A medical note on *ganja*:

Ganja (marijuana) is a mixture of leaves, stems and flowering tops of the Indian hemp plant. Though classified as a hallucinogenic drug, it is not addictive, unlike narcotics, barbiturates and alcohol. It acts mainly on the central nervous system. The effect depends on the personality of the user, the dose and the environment. The most consistent effect is a change in mood: it usually produces a sense of wellbeing, enhances self-esteem and relaxes the user. The mood changes are frequently accompanied by changes in sensory perceptions. Distances and time intervals may seem longer than they really are, as the perceptions of time and space collapse. Ordinary sounds and objects may seem aesthetically more pleasing or appealing. Sometimes it produces hallucinations, feelings of panic and psychotic episodes in persons who have no history of psychosis. It has now been proved that this is not due to individual idiosyncracies but that in high doses tetrahydrocannabinol, the active principal in *ganja*, can produce the same effect in most people.

I knew there was a good reason why the rootless at the burning ghat could not live without *ganja*. It enhances self esteem. Marx was wrong. Religion is not the opium of the people. Opium is the opium of the people.

*

Even the arrival of night has not dissuaded the peddler from pushing his magic rings. Thin brown strips of an infirm frame guard his most precious possession: a 'certificate' from the manufacturer, a Meerut resident, that these rings are indeed genuine. It is a very official-looking certificate, addressed to Someone Very Important with a Very Long address. 'I love named shopkeeper is our agent,' says the first line of the certificate. Having read O. Henry and his stories of lovelorn secretaries typing out wrong menus, I immediately recognize the error: instead of 'above named shopkeeper' the pavement artist who typed this certificate in Meerut had hammered out 'I love named shopkeeper'. When you are making a tough living at eighty words a minute, these things can be forgiven. The peddler was a pleasant young man, and quite expert at promoting the qualities of his magic ring to his audience of two men. But after a while scepticism overcame them, and they walked away. He turned to me, took one look, and decided I was a waste of time. I asked for one of the printed pamphlets, strewn on the plastic on which his wares were placed. He paused.

'Very important?' he asked.

I nodded, 'It will help'.

He gave me one. The ring, the pamphlet informed me, had been registered with the Bharat Government and was the favourite of lakhs. It destroyed every sickness, and was made of seven metals. It was a unique combination of mantras and science: '*Hamne is anguthi ko mantra shastra visheshagya duara antroccharan karte huay sundar chamchamati anguthi vaigyanik reeti se shudha saat dhatuaon ka sameekshan karke barhe parishram se banai hai.*'

He had not sold any that day. The cowries (shells) had been better for business.

*

Rani Bala...Milan Chandu Bag...,Rancha Kari Mallik...Bombaya...Chak Panchuria.. Lalit Ghosh...Sundar Nath Bairagi...Tapan Patul...Bonadi...Birati...Tunu Maity...Nani Gopal Das...For some reason people believe that a name scrawled across the wall of the crematorium is a better guarantee of salvation. Or perhaps this explanation is just a hoax, and the truth is that some of us simply cannot bear the complete obliteration of the dead, that if we cannot get the mute comfort of a grave, we can at least mark a place on the wall which will belong to us until memory eases. We are in the recess off the small plot of land on which a few pits have been dug to burn the corpses. Relatives, particularly the women, can exhaust their tears here while the pyre turns flesh to ash. It takes a good while to burn, two-and-a-half to three hours, and few people have tears that last so long. At one minute to seven, another body is set to the torch to the last fervent cries of *Hari Bol*; soon a sliver of fire is trickling down from the right corner of the old man's lips, and the mourners begin to melt quietly away in the darkness, while the *doms* shuffle the wood and ember at the bottom with bored pokes.

*

> *Manuel Flores is doomed to die.*
> *That's as sure as your money.*
> *Dying is a custom*
> *Well-known to many.*
> Borges:'Milonga of Manuel Flores.'

Well-known and never accepted. Fear consumes us, and hate of death and everything connected with it. Every untouchable is, consciously or unconsciously, reviled, but why is the *dom* hated with a particular venom? The accusations are endless: he is permanently drunk, he gambles while the dead are still burning, he haggles and extorts over the price of lighting the fire, he sells blood. Sweeper, unclean, born of the feet, and child and father of dirt. What can the *dom* do?: Death is his business, and if he had another he would gladly go to it. He too survives by the laws of supply and demand. And if he can bargain his way towards a better price, if he can pressurize you when you are secretly anxious to get over this unpleasant business of last rites, he will do it. The seth who has come to burn has cheated often enough. The babu who has come to burn has taken bribes. Ah: it is one thing to cheat the living, another to live off the dead. Death is both sacred and frightening. how could one treat it as just a matter of routine? Those who do so must be depraved, someone who is mundane about death must be malevolent, in touch with the dark, the subhuman. Inferior by birth, vile by habit. The *dom*, however, has learnt that he has a certain power which he can wield for a few minutes at each man's death, and he is not afraid to use that power, and to drink his money and die of that drink if he wants to. He will not be cowed down. You can call him a thief, a trader of corpses. He does not care. He has long stopped trying to understand your language. He knows his own and will live by that knowledge till his turn comes.

*

It is early morning and a mist lies on the river, making the pre-dawn haze more blurred. A part of the Howrah Bridge looms through the gauze, like a picture deliberately created by a photographer in search of art. The fires are out. Next to one pit, the smoke still seeping out from the charred logs, on a *charpoy*, two *doms* are sleeping — their hard, coated, dark, broken soles peeping out from under the *lewa* (Bihari shawl) covering their heads and bodies. A mud jar, which surely contained toddy last night, lies on the ground. Outside, a *dom* is stacking half burnt logs onto a cart; they will fetch some price. One *sadhu* has woken and taken his seat and begun abusing, in repetitive and unimaginative phrases, his neighbour. A few goats have started making a meal of strewn flowers, while two young men warm themselves over a smouldering pyre.

Three men are sitting around a small fire, within a small stone square near the steps to the river. I join them. One is a *sadhu* who has begun his daily quota of *ganja*. A second is young, perhaps just out of his teens, a Pandit, who spins a long yarn about being cheated when I ask him what he is doing there. The third is the colourful, jumpy one. He calls himself *siyar*, or the Jackal, and wears rings, beads, necklaces and an old pair of torn trousers around his neck. There is, near the fire, a curious pattern made of eleven match sticks: two linked squares using seven sticks, and then three matchsticks placed diagonally against the bottom side of the second square, the eleventh matchstick closing the open end. There is an unlit biri in the middle of the second square.

'What does this mean?' I ask.

The *sadhu* is silent. The young Pandit says, 'Nothing.'

The Jackal cannot restrain himself. He sways on his haunches and says excitedly, 'Can't you see? The Eleventh Hour! The Eleventh Hour!'

Tomorrow comes the bullet,
oblivion descending.
Merlin the magus said it:
being born has an ending.

Jorge Luis Borges: 'Milonga of Manuel Flores'; From *The Book of Sand*.

February 1986

The Day New Market Died

This essay moves away from the general theme of the book, social violence, but deals with a related theme — the old destroyed to make way for the new. On 12 December 1985, Calcutta's New Market died. And, with it, a part of the youth of many generations of Calcuttans, among them the author.

The warning has survived: Begging and entry of persons with communicable diseases within the premises of this market are prohibited. It is still stuck on the wooden eaves of the New Market's most popular entrance, facing the Lighthouse cinema, oblivious of the death by fire that surrounds it. I doubt if the notice ever managed to hinder anyone with a communicable disease, but the beggars were certainly kept out of the premises, converging instead on the car park in front of the Lindsay Street facade. Like everything else, beggary too was well organized, but when we spent our unemployed afternoons wandering around the New Market in the late Sixties, at least the ten-paise opera was kept within civilized limits. It had not yet become a haven of drug pushers. Yes, a few ladies who might pass on communicable diseases if care was not taken were definitely part of the scene, but that at least had none of the ugliness of the drug culture.

The entrance over which the notice hangs was the greeting-card-corner of the market. The New Market is not really a Puja or Diwali or Id shopping centre; culturally and emotionally it is a Christmas shopping centre. (The *is* came involuntarily; it is going to take time before one automatically begins to use *was* with reference to New Market.)

The night the market burnt down coincided almost precisely with the start of the Christmas season. The Christmas season — the schools begin their winter holidays, a delicious cool nip filters

down from the freezing north, schoolboys flood the maidan with
cricket, and the streets are jostling with Calcuttans walking for the
sheer pleasure of it. Christmas, as everyone knows, is not just a
Christian festival here; it is a Calcuttan celebration of joy. If the
Pujas are a time for an outpouring of the city's deep, even sublimi-
nal, passions, then its softer emotions, its sense of love and frolic
and youth create a unique effervescence during December and
Christmas.

The sparks of a civil war, limited but intense and eventually
tragic in its bloody harvest, had begun flying on College Street and
were to spread into the lanes and abrupt streets that eel their way
through Calcutta, but never, even at the height of the Naxalite
movement, was this patch of land around New Market really
touched. Christmas was always Christmas here. For us, who had
to pretend to study on College Street in the last three dramatic
years of the Sixties, this was a haven. You could sit in the Cafe de
Monico near the Metro cinema, or Karco if you had more money,
and not once hear the roar of a crashing homemade bomb through
a long conversation with a girlfriend. You could pass a happy
afternoon cruising through the maze of New Market, the uneven
corridors lined with shops radiating from the central circle; it was
never necessary to buy anything to enjoy oneself, though one
tended to avoid Nahoum's since passing that shop without stopping for a pastry was really testing the outside limits of self-control.
If it was impossible to find your way in the New Market, it was
equally impossible to get lost; you would always reach your destination (assuming you had one) even if it took a little longer than
expected. In places the market would dip, and you had to walk
down a few steps to haggle with shopkeepers who stocked nothing
but frills, their wares changing with the seasons and the festivals
and the moods. The Afghans selling dry fruits were a landmark in
the maze; it was not a very busy corner, the customers were few,
but rich; and, if memory does not deceive, there used to be a money
lender and changer nearby, his safe behind iron bars, the vermilion
swastika protecting his wealth. The cloth merchants conveyed
their superiority over less classy cloth markets like Burrabazar by
offering a Coca Cola to any woman who seemed on the point of
purchasing anything; and generally that Coca Cola sealed the deal
since the women simply got too embarrassed to change their mind

and go to another shop after having accepted the hospitality.

But our spending was, shall we say, on a more modest scale. On a good day one might invest ten paise in the weight machine to check one's fortune as much as one's weight , rarely being defeated by the fact that both turned out to be consistently depressing. And if some money had come in. then an extra *paratha roll* might be bought from across the road at Nizams' though for the accompanying Coke one strolled across to the other side: a *panwalla* near Roxy seemed to have the coldest Cokes in town. But of course the main expenditure was on the cinema ticket: Regal cinema, a little down the road, after the Corporation, for old Hindi films, particularly Dev Anand starrers; Lighthouse for the bigger hits; New Empire for the classy popular films (*Wait Until Dark* or *Dr Strangelove*); Globe for the blockbusters (*Sound of Music* et al; no movie, it seemed, came off the Globe screen, after the theatre was redecorated, before fifty weeks); and Metro really to find someone you could cadge a drink off before the night show.

Yesterday, when I went back, only Regal had not really changed: grubby as ever, the peeling walls advertised, through two-colour, overprinted posters, *Kala Pani* with the puff-creased, debonair Dev Anand and the exquisitely beautiful Madhubala in the lead. But the New Market had crashed, as if a heavy wartime raid had destroyed its enormous heart. Most of the roof had disappeared, leaving arches and columns staggered against the sky, suddenly looking like the ruins of a disappearing past. Quiet fires were licking the insides, seemingly impervious to the firemen's hoses; it was a curious combination of fire and flood, as the jet streams of water began to build up into soggy, paper heavy pools in some parts, while the fire remorselessly ate up crockery and linen and card and and plastic and snatched voraciously for more elsewhere. Those whose shops had survived the fire were hurriedly packing what they could in vans, before the now-tottering edifice broke up further. The police, looking pious after their long vigil, had ringed the area to prevent any looting; and the Army was there, just in case. A crowd had collected, of course. Calcuttans never need an excuse to stand and stare, and here was a good solid reason to do so: the heart of the city was on fire. Across the unaffected side, on the other side of Lindsay Street, were forty people who used to live inside the market, and had escaped when the heat of the conflagration woke them up. One of them had lived in the New Market for forty years. They were lucky that the fire had not started near them; everything is combustible in a place like this but they were near the dry straw and dry sacks of the poultry section. (The chickens, incidentally, survived too, but that, surely, was only a pyrrhic victory.)

There is not much point now in assigning blame — how did the short circuit arise, was the market a fire trap, why was there no water in the hydrant etc? The sad truth is that after lll years of service beyond the call of duty, age finally caught up with the New Market. The arches sloping up in prayer, the trellis and the solid brick columns, and the old man in a corner smoking a bidi, who has watched the slow or sudden shifts of political and other seasons, are now fragments of memory; they will live perhaps a shade longer where nostalgia nurtures them, and a book or two will make a niche for them in some dusty nook of a quiet library. Give way now to the future, to plastic and airconditioning, and presumably the generation currently in school and college will find romance in cement and the geometry of straight lines and clean cuts that leave no dark space cuddled against the ceiling for a pigeon to build a home. Something will come up when the bulldozers have had their say and the financiers have approved the designs in a world where life is measured by square feet.

Perhaps this is the way of destiny; perhaps God got tired of the New Market and burned it all down when we were sleeping. Or maybe all those town planners who wanted to butcher the New Market made a special application in triplicate and God answered their prayers. May I just make one plea: whatever comes up on that patch of urban excitement where we grew up, let it not be called the New Market. Call it anything you like: Marx and Lenin Market, Indira Gandhi Market, Airconditioned Market, Computerconditioned Market...Let the New Market remain the emotional possession of the old world.

December 1986

MORE ABOUT PENGUINS

For further information about books available from Penguins in India write to Penguin Books (India) Ltd, Room 2-4, 1st Floor, PTI Building, Parliament Street, New Delhi-110 001.

In the UK : For a complete list of books available from Penguins in the United Kingdom write to Dept. EP, Penguin Books Ltd, Harmondsworth, Middlesex UB 7 ODA.

In the U.S.A. : For a complete list of books available from Penguins in the United States write to Dept. DG, Penguin Books, 299 Murray Hill Parkway, East Rutherford, New Jersey 07073.

In Canada : For a complete list of books available from Penguins in Canada write to Penguin Books Canada Ltd, 2801 John Street, Markham, Ontario L3R IB4.

In Australia : For a complete list of books available from Penguins in Australia write to the Marketing Department, Penguin Books Australia Ltd, P.O. Box 257, Ringwood, Victoria 3134.

In New Zealand : For a complete list of books available from Penguins in New Zealand write to the Marketing Department, Penguin Books (N.Z.) Ltd, Private Bag, Takapuna, Auckland 9.